Editor
Gisela Lee, M.A.

Managing Editor
Karen J. Goldfluss, M.S. Ed.

Editor-in-Chief
Sharon Coan, M.S. Ed.

Illustrator
Kevin McCarthy

Cover Artist
Brenda DiAntonis

Art Manager
Kevin Barnes

Art Director
CJae Froshay

Imaging
Alfred Lau
Richard E. Easley

Product Manager
Phil Garcia

Publisher
Mary D. Smith, M.S. Ed.

Spotlight on America:
The Constitution

Author

Robert W. Smith

Teacher Created Resources, Inc.
6421 Industry Way
Westminster, CA 92683
www.teachercreated.com
ISBN: 978-0-7439-3211-0
©2004 Teacher Created Resources, Inc.
Reprinted, 2010
Made in U.S.A.

1750   1800   1850   1900   1950   2000

Table of Contents

Introduction

The Spotlight on America series is designed to introduce some of the seminal events in American history to students in the fourth through eighth grades. Reading in the content area is enriched with a balanced variety of activities in written language, social studies, and oral expression. The series is designed to make history literally come alive in your classroom and take root in the minds of your students. The reading selections and comprehension questions serve to introduce the Constitution of the United States. They set the stage for activities in other subject areas.

The Constitutional Convention was one of the great events in American history. The document it produced provides the basic law of the land for the oldest functioning democracy on earth and one of the oldest governments. The nation still functions under the separation of powers the founders devised. The legal protections against tyranny have worked well for over 200 years.

The document has proved to be both extremely sturdy and extraordinarily flexible. As Americans enter the 21st century, the Constitution has changed to meet the changing needs of the people it serves, but it has only been amended 17 times since the Bill of Rights was added in the first Congress. The government it provided has endured war, severe economic depressions, civil war, and other great crises, but the nation has survived and flourished.

The Founding Fathers who wrote the Constitution were men of great political skill and wide experience who understood the necessity of compromise. They recognized the need for a new form of government or their nation would not survive. It would fall either to internal factional fighting among states or to powerful foreign enemies. Despite a wide variety of political faiths, they carved a government which worked. Then, they convinced the people of 13 very different states to accept their creation.

The writing and oral language activities in this book are designed to help students sense the aura of crisis which surrounded the creation of the Constitution. Students should also have an understanding of the continuity and legal protections provided by the document. The research activities are intended to bring students literally into the suits and boots of people as diverse as James Madison and Edmund Randolph, George Washington and Benjamin Franklin, Alexander Hamilton and Elbridge Gerry. Many of these famous people are individuals who lived under the new form of government and shaped its earliest days. The culminating activities aim to acquaint students with the life and times of people in the new nation.

Enjoy using this book with your students and look for other books in this series.

Teacher Lesson Plans

Reading Comprehension—The Constitution of the United States

Objective: Students will demonstrate fluency and comprehension in reading historically based text.

Materials

- copies of The Constitution of the United States (pages 7–10)
- copies of The Constitution of the United States Reading Comprehension Quiz (page 31)
- additional reading selections from books, encyclopedias, and Internet sources for enrichment

Procedure

1. Reproduce and distribute The Constitution of the United States (pages 7–10). Review pre-reading skills by briefly reviewing text and encouraging students to underline as they read, make marginal notes, list questions, and highlight unfamiliar words.
2. Assign the reading as class work or homework. Allow adequate time for students to finish.
3. Talk about these discussion questions or others of your choosing with the students.
   - What does the Preamble state is the intent of the Constitution?
   - What are some of the most important features of the legislative branch of government?
   - What are some of the most important features of the executive branch of government?

Assessment—Have students complete the The Constitution of the United States Reading Comprehension Quiz (page 31). Correct and evaluate the quiz for student understanding.

· ·

Reading Comprehension—The Articles of Confederation and the Constitutional Convention

Objective: Students will demonstrate fluency and comprehension in reading historically based text.

Materials

- copies of The Articles of Confederation and The Constitutional Convention (pages 11–15)
- copies of Creating the Constitution Reading Comprehension Quiz (page 32)
- additional reading selections from books, encyclopedias, and Internet sources for enrichment

Procedure

1. Reproduce and distribute The Articles of Confederation and The Constitutional Convention (pages 11–15). Review pre-reading skills by briefly reviewing text and encouraging students to underline as they read, make marginal notes, list questions, and highlight unfamiliar words.
2. Assign the reading as class work or homework. Allow adequate time for students to finish.
3. Talk about these discussion questions or others of your choosing with the students.
   - What were the weaknesses of the Articles of Confederation?
   - What were the problems encountered by the delegates to the Constitutional Convention?
   - How did the completed Constitution differ from the Articles of Confederation?

Assessment—Have students complete Creating the Constitution Reading Comprehension Quiz (page 32). Correct and evaluate the quiz for student understanding.

Teacher Lesson Plans *(cont.)*

Reading Comprehension—The Convention Leaders

Objective: Students will demonstrate fluency and comprehension in reading historically based text.

Materials

- copies of The Convention Leaders (pages 16–19)
- copies of The Men at the Convention Reading Comprehension Quiz (page 33)
- additional reading selections from books, encyclopedias, and Internet sources for enrichment

Procedure

1. Reproduce and distribute The Convention Leaders (pages 16–19). Review pre-reading skills by briefly reviewing text and encouraging students to underline as they read, make marginal notes, list questions, and highlight unfamiliar words.

2. Assign the reading as class work or homework. Allow adequate time for students to finish.

3. Talk about these discussion questions or others of your choosing with the students.

- Who were the most important leaders at the Constitutional Convention?
- Who do you think was the single most important individual at the Convention? Why?
- Why did some delegates come late, leave early, or not attend at all?

Assessment—Have students complete The Men at the Convention Reading Comprehension Quiz (page 33). Correct and evaluate the quiz for student understanding.

• •

Reading Comprehension—Constitutional Compromises and Ratifying the Constitution

Objective: Students will demonstrate fluency and comprehension in reading historically based text.

Materials

- copies of Constitutional Compromises and Ratifying the Constitution (pages 20–24)
- copies of Constitutional Compromises and Ratifying the Constitution Reading Comprehension Quiz (page 34)
- additional reading selections from books, encyclopedias, and Internet sources for enrichment

Procedure

1. Reproduce and distribute Constitutional Compromises and Ratifying the Constitution (pages 20–24). Review pre-reading skills by briefly reviewing text and encouraging students to underline as they read, make marginal notes, list questions, and highlight unfamiliar words.

2. Assign the reading as class work or homework. Allow adequate time for students to finish.

3. Talk about these discussion questions or others of your choosing with the students.

- What were the major areas of compromise during the Constitutional Convention?
- What was the major conflict between the Northern and Southern states?
- Why was ratification by New York and Virginia critical to the success of the Constitution?

Assessment—Have students complete Constitutional Compromises and Ratification the Constitution Reading Comprehension Quiz (page 34). Correct and evaluate the quiz for student understanding.

Teacher Lesson Plans *(cont.)*

Reading Comprehension—Supreme Court Decisions and Constitutional Amendments

Objective: Students will demonstrate fluency and comprehension in reading historically based text.

Materials

- copies of Important Constitutional Decisions by the Supreme Court, and The Bill of Rights: The   First Ten Amendments, and The Later Amendments (pages 25–29)
- copies of Supreme Court Decisions Reading Comprehension Quiz (page 35)
- additional reading selections from books, encyclopedias, and Internet sources for enrichment

Procedure

1. Reproduce and distribute Important Constitutional Decisions by the Supreme Court, and The Bill of Rights: The First Ten Amendments, and The Later Amendments (pages 25–29). Review pre-reading skills by briefly reviewing text and encouraging students to underline as they read, make marginal notes, and list questions, and highlight unfamiliar words.

2. Assign the reading as class work or homework. Allow adequate time for students to finish.

3. Talk about these discussion questions or others of your choosing with the students.
   - What were the most important decisions made by the Supreme Court? Why?
   - Which amendments to the Constitution had the most influence on your personal life? Explain.
   - Why was the Bill of Rights so important in making the Constitution an effective form of government?

Assessment—Have students complete the Supreme Court Decisions Reading Comprehension Quiz (page 35). Correct and evaluate the quiz for student understanding.

The Constitution of the United States

Below is a simplified account of the seven Articles which make up the Constitution of the United States. The Preamble, quoted below, expresses the reasons for writing the document.

Underlined information has been changed by amendments or laws.

Preamble

We the People of the United States, in Order to form a more perfect Union, establish Justice, insure domestic Tranquillity, provide for the common defense, promote the general Welfare, and secure the Blessings of Liberty to ourselves and our Posterity, do ordain and establish this Constitution for the United States of America.

Article I

Legislative Branch

- Laws will be made by the Congress of the United States.
- Congress will be composed of two houses: the House of Representatives and the Senate.
- In the House of Representatives, the number of Representatives will be based on population.
- A Representative must be 25 years old and a citizen for seven years.
- A Representative must be a resident of the state he represents.
- One Representative is allocated for each 30,000 residents but each state shall have at least one representative.
- Three-fifths of the slave population will be counted for purposes of representation.
- The beginning number of Representatives in the House of Representatives will be as follows:

New Hampshire 3	Connecticut 5	Pennsylvania 8
Virginia 10	Georgia 3	Massachusetts 8
New York 6	Delaware 1	North Carolina 5
Rhode Island 1	New Jersey 4	Maryland 6
South Carolina 5		

- The House of Representatives will choose its Speaker.
- The House will have the sole power of impeachment.
- The Senate will be composed of two Senators from each state regardless of the size or population of the state.
- Senators are chosen by the State legislatures for a six-year term.
- Each Senator has one vote.
- One third of the Senators will be elected every two years.
- Senators must be at least thirty years of age and a United States citizen for nine years.
- A Senator must reside in the state from which he was elected.
- The Vice President of the United States is the President of the Senate but he may only vote in the event of a tie.
- The Senate has the sole power to try an impeachment.
- At least two-thirds of the members must vote for impeachment to achieve a conviction.

The Constitution of the United States *(cont.)*

Article I *(cont.)*

Legislative Branch *(cont.)*

- The Chief Justice of the Supreme Court shall preside over the deliberations if the President of the United States is being tried for impeachment.
- Congress shall assemble at least once a year.
- Each house of Congress will determine its own rules for procedures and be the judge of elections of its members.
- Each house shall keep a journal of its proceedings.
- Senators and Representatives shall be compensated for their services and paid by the United States treasury.
- No Senator or Representative can be appointed to any other public office during his service in Congress.
- All bills for raising taxes must originate in the House of Representatives but the Senate must also approve each bill before it becomes law.
- A two-thirds vote of both houses may be used to override a Presidential veto of a bill.
- Congress is permitted to:
    - ◆ coin money and regulate the value of money
    - ◆ collect taxes as needed for common defense and general welfare
    - ◆ pay debts
    - ◆ borrow money on the credit of the United States
    - ◆ regulate commerce with foreign nations and among the states
    - ◆ establish uniform rules for becoming a naturalized citizen
    - ◆ establish uniform laws about bankruptcies
    - ◆ fix national standards of weights and measures
    - ◆ establish post offices and post roads
    - ◆ guarantee exclusive rights to authors and inventors for a specific time period
    - ◆ define and punish piracy and other crimes on the high seas
    - ◆ declare war
    - ◆ raise and support armies and maintain a navy
    - ◆ call forth the militia to execute the laws of the United States and to suppress insurrections and repel invasions

- Congress may not:
    - ◆ prohibit the importation of slaves before 1808
    - ◆ suspend the writ of Habeas Corpus except in cases of rebellion or invasion where public safety may require it
    - ◆ give preference to one state over another in regulation of commerce
    - ◆ grant a title of nobility

- No state may:
    - ◆ make treaties
    - ◆ coin money
    - ◆ grant a title of nobility
    - ◆ suspend debts
    - ◆ create Bills of Credit
    - ◆ levy import or export duties or taxes
    - ◆ declare war
    - ◆ keep troops or ships of war without the consent of Congress

The Constitution of the United States *(cont.)*

Article I *(cont.)*

Legislative Branch *(cont.)*

- No person holding an office can accept a present, office, or title from a foreign state, prince, or king without the consent of Congress.
- The president must sign all laws passed by Congress or the law must be passed again by Congress by a two-thirds majority in each house to override the Presidential veto.

Article II

Executive Branch

- The president is the executive head of government. He is responsible for enforcement of the laws.
- The president is elected for a term of 4 years.
- He must be a natural-born citizen, at least 35 years of age, and a resident in the United States for at least 14 years.
- The president can be removed from office if he is impeached and convicted of treason, bribery, or other high crimes and misdemeanors.
- He is Commander in Chief of the Armed Forces.
- The president will:
    - ✦ faithfully carry out the laws of the U.S.
    - ✦ report to Congress on the "State of the Union" at regular intervals and recommend action by Congress
    - ✦ appoint the judges of the Supreme Court with the advice and consent of the Senate
    - ✦ appoint ambassadors to foreign nations
    - ✦ make treaties with foreign nations with the approval of two-thirds of the Senate
    - ✦ (may) pardon individuals for offenses against the United States

Article III

Judicial Branch

- There will be one Supreme Court and such lesser courts as the Congress may establish.
- Judges of the Supreme Court will hold office for life during good behavior.
- The Supreme Court will try all cases which have to do with the Constitution and the laws of the United States.
- All persons accused of crimes may be tried by a jury except in an impeachment.
- U.S. courts may hear suits between states and citizens of different states as well as suits by foreign countries or individuals.
- Courts shall try cases having to do with crime on the high seas.
- Treason is waging war on the United States or giving aid and comfort to the enemies of the United States.
- Conviction for treason requires either a personal confession in open court or testimony of two witnesses to the same act.
- Congress has the power to declare the punishment for treason.

The Constitution of the United States (cont.)

Article IV

Relationship of States to Each Other

- Each state will respect the laws of all other states.
- Citizens of one state enjoy the privileges of citizens in all states.
- Persons charged in a crime who flee from a state must be returned to the state they fled from.
- The federal government guarantees protection to states against foreign invasion and against local violence, if it overcomes the resources of the state.
- The United States will guarantee each state a republican form of government [meaning an elected representative government].
- New states will be admitted to the Union but they will not be formed from the territory of existing states without the consent of the existing states and the Congress.

Article V

Amending the Constitution

- Congress shall propose amendments when two-thirds of both houses decide it is necessary or when the legislatures of two-thirds of all the states decide it is necessary.
- In either case, a proposed amendment must be ratified by the legislatures of three-fourths of all the states.
- An amendment which is ratified is a valid part of the Constitution.
- An amendment may not deprive a state of its right of representation in the Senate.

Article VI

The Supreme Law of the Land

- The United States under the Constitution shall assume responsibility for all debts and treaties entered into under the Articles of Confederation.
- The Constitution, the laws made under the Constitution, and treaties entered into, shall be the supreme law of the land.
- All Senators, Representatives, judges, and members of State legislatures must swear an oath to support the Constitution.
- No religious requirement can be made as a qualification to hold any public office.

Article VII

Ratification

- The Constitution shall become valid and take effect when ratified by nine of the thirteen states.

The Articles of Confederation

A League of States

The Articles of Confederation created by the Continental Congress, established the goverment of the U.S. In 1778 a committee of the Continental Congress proposed the Articles and they took effect in 1781 after the 13th state, Maryland, ratified them. In reality, the Articles were only a league of friendship between and among states. They created a confederation of 13 sovereign, independent states in a voluntary league of states. Each state had total independence and self-rule.

Weak Government

The Articles of Confederation created a weak and ineffective national government. George Washington described the government under the Articles of Confederation as "a half-starved limping government, that appears to be always moving upon crutches and tottering at every step." The organization of the government had a one-chamber Congress in which each state had one vote. Every action required the support of 9 of the 13 states for approval.

No Taxes/No Money

The national government under the Articles had no money and no authority to impose or collect taxes. It could not make trade agreements with other nations. Each state made its own agreements, independent of any concerns for other states or the nation. The federal government was not permitted to regulate trade between the states. States with good seaports imposed taxes on goods from other states which came into their ports. These taxes were a burden to merchants in states without ports. Each state had its own tariff laws (taxes on goods coming from or being shipped to other countries), just as nations do.

Public Order

The national government could not enforce public order. Each state had its own local militia. The national government could not create an army or a navy. Therefore, the United States had no military force to enforce its rights in dealing with other nations. There were many problems with other nations. Spain, which owned Florida and the city of New Orleans and other southern land areas, would not allow American farmers in the west to ship their goods down the Mississippi River to New Orleans to be shipped to other nations. Britain had signed the Treaty of Paris in 1783 but refused to abide by parts of the agreement. For example, they insisted on leaving fur trading posts in New York.

The Articles of Confederation *(cont.)*

High Debts

There were severe economic and financial problems in the nation. The United States owed money to other nations which they had borrowed during the Revolutionary War. They were unable to pay a war debt of over 12 million dollars to foreign nations.

The national government had more than 40 million dollars in domestic debt as well. The states also had a total of about 25 million dollars in debt. Individual creditors were forced to sell repayment notes at low prices. Other countries considered the United States as having no financial future.

Worthless Money

In addition, people owed money to state governments. There were at least a dozen different local currencies and some foreign currencies as well. To meet the problem of a money shortage, some states printed worthless paper money. Other states used British currency and a few states used Spanish dollars. Although the idea of a simplified central decimal currency had been proposed by Thomas Jefferson and supported by many in the Congress, there was no way to back up the money with so many states destitute and the central government powerless to collect taxes.

Farmers in Trouble

Farmers were hit especially hard and their land was highly taxed in some states. Taxes placed on farmland were expected to be paid in cash, but there was very little cash to be earned. Farmers had almost no cash and were often paid with bartered goods rather than cash which was in such short supply. Debtors (people who owed money) were often thrown into prison until their debts were paid. This made matters even worse because they had no opportunity to grow their crops or earn any other money in prison.

Shays' Rebellion

Shays' Rebellion in Massachusetts was a reaction to this situation. In the mid-1770s, farmers were losing their property and facing jail time due to their debts. In 1786 and 1787, Daniel Shays led a group of poor farmers in the state who were ready to protest and fight against the taxes. They stormed local courthouses and even a federal arsenal. The rebellion had to be put down with force by local militias. The rebellion led to near chaos in Boston and caused panic in many states with similar problems. States and the national government were both fearful of mob violence.

National Solutions Needed

National solutions were needed to address these national problems. A new strong national government was needed rather than a weak association of states. The Constitution of the United States was written to meet these needs and solve the problems of the Articles of the Confederation.

The Constitutional Convention

Getting Started

Since 1781 the United States had been governed under the Articles of Confederation, but the government wasn't working very well. A convention of states dealing with interstate commerce met in Annapolis in 1786 and proposed that a convention be held the next year to deal with some of the deficiencies of the Confederation. The states agreed to a convention to revise the Articles of Confederation to be held in Philadelphia in May 1787. The idea had been discussed for several years because many public leaders had observed and discussed the failures of the existing government.

Due to travel problems and the uncertain response of many states, only Virginia and Pennsylvania had delegates present on the appointed day of May 14. Gradually, delegates arrived and on May 25, 1787, the Constitutional Convention formally opened in what is now Independence Hall in Philadelphia. By the end of the convention, 12 of the 13 states sent delegates. Rhode Island would have nothing to do with the deliberations. A total of 55 delegates attended the convention at some time, and 39 signed the document.

The Delegates

George Washington was immediately elected president of the convention. Important leaders at the convention included Benjamin Franklin, as a representative from Pennsylvania and Gouverneur Morris who "wrote" the final document in his handwriting. James Madison, called the "Father of the Constitution," kept notes, delivered speeches, and helped formulate several compromises. Other important men included Roger Sherman, Edmund Randolph, and Alexander Hamilton.

Important Americans who didn't attend included Thomas Jefferson and John Adams who were overseas serving as ambassadors. Patrick Henry refused to attend, and 18 others who were chosen by their states couldn't or wouldn't attend. A total of 74 delegates were appointed and 55 attended.

The Rules

The delegates agreed to some ground rules. Only delegates would be allowed to attend meetings. There would be no visitors and no reporters. Sentries were actually placed at the doors to insure that deliberations were kept secret. The windows were closed to prevent eavesdropping.

The delegates quickly agreed on the need to devise a new form of government, not just to revise the Articles of Confederation. Most delegates wanted a strong, firm, central government that still had to respect the rights of the people and the individual character of the states. The problems at the convention centered around how to accomplish this purpose.

The Constitutional Convention *(cont.)*

Problems

Conflicts arose between the rural South with its large plantation-style farming economy and the North with its shipping interests and small farmers. Slavery became an important and divisive issue between the Northern and Southern states. Southerners used slaves on their plantations while slavery was dying out in most Northern states. There was also deep distrust between the smaller states and the large states. The small states feared they would be dominated by the larger states and the large states didn't want their interests thwarted by the smaller ones. Important compromises would address these issues.

Conditions

The summer heat of Philadelphia was oppressive as the delegates labored to find effective compromises which would produce a Constitution that most Americans would accept. Bluebottle flies were everywhere and harassed the delegates with their constant buzzing.

The Document

The framers approved the Constitution on September 15, 1787, and formally signed it on the 17th. The Constitution contains the nation's basic framework of laws. It establishes the form and shape of our national government. The document defines the rights and liberties of the people and limits the authority of the federal government over states and people. Federal powers include the right to raise taxes, to create an army, to declare war, and to regulate trade. Many powers are denied to the federal government and are restricted to the states or to the people. The Constitution's original form had a preamble and seven articles. (It now has 27 amendments which have been added since 1791.)

The Constitution establishes a federal system of government with three branches: legislative, executive, and judicial. The legislative branch has two houses of Congress—a House of Representatives based on population, and a Senate with two Senators from each state. The executive branch is comprised of the President of the United States and all of the administrative offices under his control. The judicial branch is comprised of the Supreme Court with nine members (at present) who serve for life. The three branches allow for the separation of powers so that no one branch of government and no one person can exercise authoritarian control. This system of checks and balances ensures that no branch of government is able to dominate the others.

The Constitutional Convention *(cont.)*

Above All Government Powers

The rule of law expressed in the Constitution was placed above all laws and all institutions. The Congress and the president must abide by the law, just as all other individuals and government representatives must. This feature had not existed in English law where the king often considered himself above the law.

A Rising Sun

When Ben Franklin approached the table to sign the Constitution, he gestured to the half sun painted on the back of Washington's convention chair. He said that throughout the months of deliberations, he had been unable to decide if it was a rising or a setting sun. The final document convinced him that it was a rising sun, a good symbol for his country.

Ratification

Each state held its own ratification convention. The issues were widely debated in newspapers, pamphlets, public debates, and in the conventions. Arguments for and against the Constitution made the vote very close in two key states, Virginia and New York, but the proponents of the new government prevailed in the end.

New Government

In January 1789 presidential electors were selected by legislatures or direct vote of the people in 10 of the states which had ratified the Constitution. (New York did not send them. North Carolina and Rhode Island had not yet ratified.)

On February 4, 1789, the presidential electors selected George Washington as president. The first Congress met on March 4, 1789, and President Washington was inaugurated on April 30, 1789.

A Bill of Rights

Rhode Island and North Carolina refused to ratify the Constitution until a Bill of Rights was included. Many other states ratified only on condition that a Bill of Rights be added. James Madison took the lead in getting congressional approval for 12 amendments to the Constitution. By the end of 1791, enough states had approved 10 of these amendments which are known as the Bill of Rights. These amendments protected freedom of speech, the right to assemble peaceably, freedom of religion, the right to bear arms, and the right to trial by jury.

Amendments

Today there are 27 amendments—the original 10 and 17 others. An amendment may be proposed by a two-thirds majority of both houses of Congress or by a national convention called for by two-thirds of the state legislatures. It must be ratified either by three-fourths of the state legislatures or by conventions in three-fourths of the states.

The Convention Leaders

When Thomas Jefferson heard who was attending the Constitutional Convention, he called it "an assembly of demigods" because the members were so rich in education and political experience. These practical national leaders were often successful businessmen as well. The list of occupations included merchants, lawyers, army officers, plantation owners, judges, financiers, politicians, farmers, doctors, and even a shoemaker.

At a time when a college education was an opportunity for only a tiny fraction of the populace, almost half of the delegates were college educated. There were four graduates of Yale, four from William and Mary, three from Harvard, two from Columbia, and eight from Princeton. Some had been educated in Europe and several others had little formal education but were self-taught. The delegates were well read in the classics of Greece and Rome and were familiar with the latest political ideas and intellectual discussions.

Thirty-nine of the 55 delegates had served in Congress under the Articles of Confederation. A few of the delegates had helped write their new state constitutions, and many had served in their state legislatures or as officers in the state. Seven of the delegates had been or were governors of their states. Nearly half had fought in the Revolutionary War, and eight of the delegates had signed the Declaration of Independence.

Fifty-five delegates attended the convention at one time or another and 39 delegates signed the document. Although each state had only one vote in the proceedings, states had various numbers of delegates. New Hampshire had two delegates, Massachusetts four, Connecticut three, New York three, New Jersey five, Pennsylvania eight, Delaware five, Maryland five, Virginia seven, North Carolina five, South Carolina four, and Georgia four. Rhode Island refused to send anyone.

HAMILTON

RANDOLPH

MADISON

FRANKLIN

WASHINGTON

The Convention Leaders *(cont.)*

James Madison

The most important member of the convention was the 36-year-old scholarly lawyer from Virginia who became known as the "Father of the Constitution." The shortest man at the convention, the five feet four inches Princeton graduate studiously prepared for his role. He had previous experience as a member of the Virginia legislature and as a member of Congress under the Articles of Confederation.

Madison arrived in Philadelphia nearly three weeks early armed with books and ideas. At his request, his friend Thomas Jefferson had sent him hundreds of books dealing with history, types of government, law, ancient civilizations, and modern nations. He studied John Adams' new book on constitutions. He analyzed all forms of government, took notes, and wrote suggestions.

Madison's studies confirmed his thinking about the need for a new form of a strong, national government with supremacy over the states. He believed such a government would reduce economic and social differences between the states, even differences over slavery. Most historians believe that he was the principal author of the Virginia Plan which became the basic concept around which the Constitution was framed. Even before the convention started, he devised the system of ratification that would be used to achieve acceptance of the Constitution.

Never absent from the proceedings, James Madison always sat in front of the convention and took extensive notes on almost all speeches, arguments, and discussions. He argued strenuously for ratification and was the author of at least 26 of The Federalist Papers in support of ratification. In the new government, Madison became a congressman and chairman of the committee that wrote the amendments which became known as the Bill of Rights. Later he served as Secretary of State and President of the United States.

Benjamin Franklin

Benjamin Franklin, at 81 the oldest delegate to the convention and in poor health, arrived at the Philadelphia State House in a Chinese sedan chair carried by four prisoners from the city jail. An internationally renowned scientist and inventor, Franklin had only recently returned from France. Wealthy and very influential throughout the colonies and in his adopted state of Pennsylvania, Franklin was the presiding officer of the Pennsylvania delegation.

Franklin had long supported a strong national government. As early as 1754, he proposed the Albany Plan of Union to create such a government. Ben Franklin had signed the Declaration of Independence and the Treaty of Paris. He had negotiated the alliance with France which was essential to the success of the war for American independence.

Franklin had a reputation for witty and charming conversation. Because he gave many dinner parties, someone from the convention always attended and stayed near Franklin to make sure he never gave away any secret details or convention gossip. They merely diverted the conversation.

Franklin was often ill and did not actually speak much at the convention, but his diplomatic comments and shrewd common sense often helped to diffuse anger and support compromise. Although Franklin was widely admired, he was not always listened to. Among other suggestions, he supported unpaid public servants and a one-house legislature. He said the Constitution wasn't perfect but that it needed to be given a chance.

The Convention Leaders *(cont.)*

George Washington

George Washington, the 55-year-old Virginia planter who had led his country through eight years of war as Commander-in-Chief of the revolutionary army, was famous throughout the nation and widely regarded as the "Father of his Country." Washington's presence and influence were essential to the success of the convention.

The presiding officer of the convention, Washington was fair and impartial and rarely allowed his personal feelings to show. In private discussions, he was a forceful advocate for a strong central government and an effective voice for compromise. He feared sectional conflict and rivalries among the individual states. He had been often frustrated by the failures of the Continental Congress to provide adequate pay and supplies for his army, and he knew that many of these deficiencies resulted from the inherent weakness of Congress.

Alexander Hamilton

Hamilton had been Washington's military aide and close friend during the war. An immigrant from the West Indies, he graduated from Columbia University and practiced law in New York where he had also been a delegate to Congress under the Articles of Confederation. The 30-year-old Hamilton had supported the idea of a Constitutional Convention since 1780. He had attended the Annapolis Trade Convention which recommended a convention to revise the Articles of Confederation.

Alexander Hamilton favored an extremely powerful central government. He disliked the idea of "sovereign states" which he perceived as weak and jealous of each other. Hamilton wanted a strong chief executive with many powers usually associated with kings. He suggested a lifetime term for the president who would have absolute veto power over congressional laws.

The other two delegates from New York never voted to support Hamilton's suggestions and left the convention because they didn't approve of the new form of government. Hamilton came and went but did sign the document and support its ratification. He wrote at least 51 of The Federalist Papers and was influential in convincing New Yorkers to ratify the Constitution. New York's support was considered crucial to success due to its location and size. Hamilton was killed in a duel with Aaron Burr in 1804.

Edmund Randolph

Randolph was the governor of Virginia and a major leader of the Virginia delegation. He presented the Virginia Plan, a resolution to create a new form of government rather than revise the Articles of Confederation. He was an effective speaker and participant. He refused to sign the final document because it lacked a Bill of Rights, but he did work effectively for ratification.

The Convention Leaders *(cont.)*

Gouverneur Morris

A 35-year-old Columbia graduate, Morris was born into a wealthy family. His fondness for racing horses had cost him a leg but did not seem to slow him down. He had signed the Articles of Confederation as a delegate from New York and served in the Continental Congress. Morris later moved to Pennsylvania and was a convention member from that state. Morris was an outstanding speaker and made as many speeches as Madison. He favored a strong central government and wanted property qualifications for voting and holding office. Morris actually wrote much of the document as a member of the Committee of Style and Arrangement.

George Mason

A 62-year-old aristocratic planter and colonel in the Revolutionary army, Mason was an important voice in the convention and an intense believer in democracy. He opposed counting slaves for the House of Representatives and wanted to curtail the slave trade. He insisted that the House have the power to initiate tax bills. The author of Virginia's Declaration of Rights, he wanted a Bill of Rights in the document and left the convention, refusing to sign the Constitution when it was not added.

John Dickinson

Dickinson, a 55-year-old lawyer and scholar who had been governor of both Pennsylvania and Delaware, represented Delaware at the convention. He was famous as a revolutionary activist and author of *The Letters from a Farmer in Pennsylvania* in which he attacked British taxation without representation. He was chairman of the committee which wrote the Articles of Confederation. He particularly feared domination by the large states.

Roger Sherman

A 56-year-old Connecticut lawyer, judge, and member of Congress who had signed the Declaration of Independence and the Articles of Confederation, Sherman feared democracy. He felt the common people were stupid and easily misled. He was a poor speaker with a strong Yankee accent who was not too popular with the other delegates. He was fearful of domination by the large states. He saw no reason for a Bill of Rights.

Elbridge Gerry

A 43-year-old wealthy Massachusetts merchant with a Harvard education, Gerry was a consistent opponent of a strong national government and a permanent national army. Although he had signed both the Declaration of Independence and the Articles of Confederation, he feared too much democracy and election by the people. Nonetheless, he wanted frequent yearly elections for the House of Representatives but a fifteen-year presidential term. He left the convention and did not sign the Constitution because it lacked a Bill of Rights.

Constitutional Compromises

Big States Versus Small States

The weaknesses of the Articles of Confederation were known to all serious observers in 1787. The problem for the delegates to the Constitutional Convention was what to do about them. The primary sticking point at the convention developed over the conflict between large states and small states. The large states were Virginia, Pennsylvania, and Massachusetts. Together they represented half the population of the United States. Each of them was more than ten times larger by population than Rhode Island, New Jersey, or Delaware. Georgia and the Carolinas, states with large land areas, were expected to rapidly increase in population. New York, Connecticut, and New Hampshire had small populations compared to Virginia and Pennsylvania.

The essence of the conflict was this: The large states believed that the new government should have proportional representation based on the number of people in a state. The Virginia Plan and its leaders, such as James Madison, thought it was undemocratic and unfair for the few voters of Delaware, for example, to have an equal vote with the many voters of Virginia. They perceived this as one of the fundamental flaws of the Articles of Confederation.

The small states were adamant that they would not be overwhelmed by the large states. They believed that their interests would not be protected and the new government would be run solely for the convenience of the large states. This issue nearly dissolved the convention. However, Roger Sherman proposed a Connecticut Compromise which suggested that every state have two votes—one based on population and one with each state equally represented. Years before he had proposed a similar idea for the Articles of Confederation but it was rejected.

This idea, which led to a House of Representatives based on population and a Senate with two votes from each state regardless of size, was ultimately accepted, although the voting was very close. The complete absence of Rhode Island from the convention and the failure of New Hampshire delegates to arrive would have given the large states a six to five majority but at the critical moment an almost unknown member from Maryland named Daniel of Saint Thomas Jenifer, a close friend of George Washington, deliberately stayed away from the convention so that his colleague Luther Martin could cast Maryland's vote with the smaller states. Georgia's vote would still have given the large states a majority but Abraham Baldwin, a representative of Georgia who was born in Connecticut, canceled the vote of the other Georgia delegate leaving a five–five tie. Intelligent members of the convention from other big states realized the smaller states had to have this compromise and one by one rose to accept it. In many ways, this is a model of how American government still works.

Constitutional Compromises (cont.)

Northern States vs. Southern States

The conflict between the smaller states and the larger states served to make the most observant members of the convention realize that the deeper issues really hinged on the differences between Northern and Southern interests. Northerners were often traders and ship builders who transported Southern farm crops, such as tobacco, rice, cotton, and sugar to other countries. The rural Southerners had a large slave population, but slavery was rapidly declining in the North because it wasn't very useful in economic terms and because Northern religious leaders often opposed it.

Northern delegates realized that Southern delegates had to protect slavery if their states were to accept the Constitution, but they used it as a bargaining chip to get some concessions for their states. When the bargaining was completed, there were five basic agreements.

1. Slavery would not be allowed in the new states which would develop in the Northwest Territory. All or part of six states would be formed from this territory—Illinois, Ohio, Indiana, Michigan, Wisconsin, and Minnesota.
2. Slaves could still be imported for the next 20 years until 1808. After that the issue was up to Congress to settle.
3. Export taxes, which were hated by Southern planters as well as some Northern businessmen, were forbidden. The federal and state governments would have to find other sources of revenue.
4. Three-fifths of the slaves in a state would be counted for the purposes of representation in Congress and for taxation. This "Three-fifth's Compromise" benefited the Southern states.
5. Southern slave owners would be permitted to search for runaway slaves in Northern states. This issue would lead to intense anger and conflict in the next 70 years.

The Presidency

There was intense disagreement over the nature of the presidency. Some members wanted a very strong president with almost king-like tenure and powers. Alexander Hamilton wanted a president with a very long term or even a lifetime appointment with a veto over most legislation. Others wanted a president elected to a brief one or two-year term who had little control over legislation. Ultimately, they agreed upon a president with strong powers elected to a four-year term and able to be reelected.

Separation of Powers

The members allowed the president to veto legislation, but they also allowed the Congress to override a veto with a two-thirds majority of both houses. They invented a Supreme Court to keep a check on the powers of both the president and Congress. The court also became an arbiter of difficult issues in the law.

Ratifying the Constitution

Getting Started

Writing the Constitution was enormously difficult. Getting it approved by the individual states was even harder. The delegates left the convention proud of their work, in most cases, but aware that they had a huge job ahead of them to convince the voters in their states to ratify the document.

The existing Confederation Congress meeting in New York immediately began the process leading to ratification. On September 28, 1787, just 11 days after the document was signed in Philadelphia, Congress asked the legislature of each state to submit the new plan of government to a convention for approval or rejection.

Publication of the document immediately provoked a widespread and spirited discussion of the proposed new government. Opposition to the constitution was very strong in some states and it is generally agreed that more people actually opposed the new government than favored it.

Supporters and Opponents

Opposition was especially strong from the groups which were already afraid of the existing state and national governments. Poor farmers and other rural citizens distrusted any strong government. They remembered their experiences with British rule and feared a new government would become just as difficult. Debtors were especially fearful of a stronger government.

Supporters of the new plan often included big city businessmen, craftsmen, workers, and many large landowners who believed that a more efficient government would provide better protection and more opportunities for business to succeed.

Political supporters of the new plan were called the Federalists. They were disgusted with the weaknesses inherent in the Articles of Confederation. They felt the new nation was at the mercy of foreign nations and that financial ruin was likely due to the difficulty in raising revenue and paying war debts. They wanted a strong central government which the Constitution provided.

The opposition, who became known as Anti-Federalists, feared a strong central government or the emergence of a government which could exert force as the British government had done. They had just fought a revolution against one oppressive tyranny. They didn't want another. They were especially upset that no Bill of Rights was included in the document.

Ratifying the Constitution *(cont.)*

The Federalist Papers

The intellectual and political ideas at the center of the debate over ratification are expressed in The Federalist Papers, a series of 85 essays which provided the reasons for creating the new government and the rationale for supporting the Constitution. Written by James Madison, Alexander Hamilton, and John Jay, they were designed to sway public opinion in support of the document, especially in New York where opposition was strong.

The papers were each signed with the pseudonym "Publius" and published in local papers. Beginning on October 27, 1787, the essays detailed the many failures of the government as it operated under the Articles of Confederation and outlined the strengths and improvements in the new Constitution. The authors admitted that the Constitution wasn't perfect and that compromises were necessary if a united nation was to be created. The Federalist Papers were widely reprinted and read throughout the states. These were among the most important reasons for eventual ratification by the states.

Discussion and Debate

All of the arguments of the delegates at the Constitutional Convention were revisited by delegates to the state conventions, in the newspapers, and in public discussions. Resentments against other states, hatred of slavery and fear of domination by slave states in the North, fear of Northern opposition to slavery in the South, and distrust of large states by small states were all widely discussed.

The issue of a Bill of Rights was a real stumbling block for many delegates. It was widely perceived as a serious failure that one was not included with the document. Even many loyal supporters felt obliged to admit the problem and suggest that it had to be among the first pieces of business in the new government.

State by State

Nonetheless, some states recognized that it was the best chance for success and the best deal they were likely to get. Delaware was the first to ratify on December 7, 1787, with the unanimous consent of their ratifying convention.

Pennsylvania voted on December 12 to ratify the Constitution, but it also had the unenviable distinction of having the most violent process. Two Anti-Federalist members of the Pennsylvania assembly were actually forced by a mob to attend a meeting which was voting on a ratification convention. James Wilson, a leading Anti-Federalist, was beaten after ratification by opponents armed with clubs.

Ratifying the Constitution *(cont.)*

The States Approve

New Jersey's convention unanimously approved the document on December 18, 1787. Georgia ratified on January 2, 1788. Connecticut ratified on January 9, 1788. On February 6 the Massachusetts convention narrowly approved the document. Maryland voted for ratification on April 28. South Carolina approved on May 23.

The Critical States

But the two critical states were Virginia and New York. The physical size, the location, and large population of Virginia made it essential to the success of the new nation. New York's location and large physical area also made it a key state.

In Virginia the arguments were heated and the debates very intense. George Washington wrote letters to friends and supporters of the document. James Madison, John Marshall, and war hero "Light Horse Harry" Lee led the Federalists. Edmund Randolph, who had not signed the document as a delegate because it lacked a Bill of Rights, still supported it at the state level.

Patrick Henry was relentlessly opposed to any strong central government. He felt the Articles of Confederation were just fine because they did hamstring the government and prevent the kind of abuses suffered under the rule of King George III.

On June 25, 1788, Virginia ratified the Constitution in a close vote. They also recommended some amendments, including a Bill of Rights.

New York was the last major stumbling block. Sentiment was really strongly opposed to ratification in New York and had Virginia not approved of the new government, neither would have New York. But passage in Virginia and the strong support of leaders such as Alexander Hamilton and John Jay gradually swayed some delegates. The opposition leaders, Governor Clinton and Melancton Smith, had no better alternatives to suggest.

Then news arrived that New Hampshire had ratified on June 21, 1788. They had been the ninth state to ratify. Only nine states were needed to put the Constitution into effect and Virginia had also ratified to become the 10th state. The vote was close and the debate was fierce, but New York finally approved on July 26, 1788. North Carolina came on board in November of 1789, and Rhode Island finally approved in May 1790. The Constitution was the law of the land.

Important Constitutional Decisions by the Supreme Court

A Living Document

The Constitution has faced many challenges in the two centuries since it has been in force. Many of the early challenges were related to the issue of slavery and where it would be allowed. The Missouri Compromise of 1820 and the Compromise of 1850 were both attempts to deal with this problem. The Civil War would finally resolve that issue.

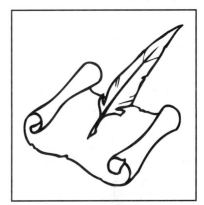

Most challenges to the Constitution were resolved by the Supreme Court as it interpreted the document and the intent of the Founding Fathers in the light of the times in which they lived. These are some of the most important decisions of the Court.

1803 Marbury v. Madison

This case involved an appointment by President John Adams of a justice of the peace in Washington, D. C., just before President Jefferson took office. Adams' appointee, William Marbury, was refused his commission by the new president and sued the new Secretary of State James Madison to receive his commission.

Congress had given the Supreme Court the right to review such procedures. Chief Justice John Marshall ruled against Marbury on the basis that the Supreme Court had no right to hear the case because Congress had passed a law which was not allowed by the Constitution. In his ruling, Marshall established the right of the Supreme Court to judicial review which involves the right to declare a law unconstitutional. It was a critical ruling because it helped establish the independence of the Supreme Court.

Other Early Decisions

John Marshall intended to build the power of the court to make it an equal branch of government with the presidency and Congress. Chief Justice Marshall served from 1801 to 1835. He was a man with wide experience in government, an officer during the American Revolution, and had been deeply involved in getting Virginia to ratify the Constitution.

In *Gibbons v. Ogden*, Marshall's ruling prohibited states from interfering with interstate commerce. In an 1819 ruling on a decision entitled *McCulloch v. Maryland*, he stated that the Congress possessed "implied powers," beyond those specifically stated in the Constitution. He clearly established in this and other decisions that federal laws, such as treaties, took precedence over state laws, and that state laws which violated federal statutes were unconstitutional and may not be enforced.

Important Constitutional Decisions
by the Supreme Court *(cont.)*

The Dred Scott Decision

Roger Taney became Chief Justice after the death of Marshall and led the
Court from 1835 until his death in 1864. He too firmly enhanced the power
of the Supreme Court. However, he is responsible for one of the most
notorious decisions of the Court. Dred Scott, a slave, was brought by his
owner to Illinois and the Wisconsin Territory.

Scott sued for his freedom on the grounds that he should have been set free
once he entered states or territories which forbid slavery. Taney and several
of his fellow judges believed that the states had the power to maintain
slavery or to free slaves. On this issue of states rights, Taney's court differed
with the court under John Marshall.

In this decision Taney made two rulings which would ultimately lead to civil
war. He ruled that slaves were property and thus Scott was not a citizen and couldn't sue in court.
Secondly, the Court ruled that Congress could not prohibit slavery in territories, such as Wisconsin,
which were not yet states. This ruling essentially outlawed the Missouri Compromise which had
established some free states. Without Congressional power to mandate free or slave states, compromise
between the North and South became far more difficult. Dred Scott, purchased by a new owner, was
given his freedom two months after the court decision.

Plessy v. Ferguson

In the aftermath of the Civil War, the passage of the 13th, 14th, and 15th Amendments was designed to
provide equality under the law for African Americans. However, an 1896 ruling by the court
interpreted the Constitution as allowing "separate but equal" facilities for blacks and whites. This
ruling condemned African Americans to almost 60 years of second-class citizenship as they were forced
to use separate means of transportation, schools, dining rooms, inns, and even water fountains.

Other decisions in the late 1800s tended to support the rights of corporations over those of individuals
and the states. Court decisions became gradually less one-sided in the early 1900s.

Brown v. Board of Education

In 1951 an African American father sued the school board of Topeka, Kansas, because he wanted his
daughter to attend the all-white school nearer to his home. The most important decision of modern
times was the ruling in 1954 which stated that "separate but equal" schools were unconstitutional. This
decision led to the gradual desegregation of public schools, buses, hotels, restaurants, and other public
places.

The Bill of Rights: The First Ten Amendments

Below is a simplified explanation of each amendment.

Amendment I

Congress may not set up any religious organization or interfere with religious freedom. Congress cannot limit the right of free speech or free press or the right of people to peacefully assemble and petition the government to correct their grievances (complaints).

Amendment II

The people have the right to own and carry firearms.

Amendment III

People cannot be forced to house and feed soldiers in peacetime and only if special laws are passed in time of war.

Amendment IV

People may not be personally searched or seized, nor have their possessions searched or seized, without a warrant and reasonable cause to believe a crime has been committed by the person charged.

Amendment V

A grand jury is provided for serious crimes. A person cannot be tried twice for the same crime and a person cannot be forced to testify in criminal cases against himself. A person cannot be deprived of life, liberty, or property without due process of law.

Amendment VI

A person is entitled to a fair, speedy, public trial by jury. A person is entitled to know the charges against him, to confront witnesses against him, to call witnesses for himself, and to obtain the advice of a lawyer.

Amendment VII

A jury trial is permitted in civil suits where the value exceeds $20.

Amendment VIII

People may not be subjected to excessive bail or fines nor to cruel and unusual punishments.

Amendment IX

The listing of some rights in the Constitution does not limit or deny other rights not specifically mentioned.

Amendment X

All powers not specifically given to the United States by the Constitution or forbidden to the states are reserved to the states or to the people.

| 1750 | 1800 | 1850 | 1900 | 1950 | 2000 |

The Later Amendments

Below is a brief summation of each of the last 17 amendments.

[The information in brackets briefly explains the reasons for some amendments.]

Amendment XI (Proposed 1794 – Ratified 1798)

Citizens of one state may not sue another state in United States courts and citizens of a foreign country may not sue a state in United States courts.

Amendment XII (Proposed 1804 – Ratified 1804)

Provides for separate ballots for electors of the president and vice president. The president and vice president may not be from the same state. The House of Representatives will select the president from the top contenders if no candidate has a majority. [Previously the vice president had received the next highest number of votes and was usually the political opponent of the president.]

Amendment XIII (Proposed 1865 – Ratified 1865)

Slavery and involuntary servitude are forbidden in the United States except imprisonment for a crime. [This and the next two amendments providing citizenship to former slaves were a result of Northern victory in the Civil War.]

Amendment XIV (Proposed 1866 – Ratified 1868)

States may not limit the citizenship rights of any person or deprive anyone of life, liberty, or property without due process of law. [This was designed to protect former slaves.]

Amendment XV (Proposed 1869 – Ratified 1870)

No citizen can be prevented from voting in state or federal elections because of his race, color, or previous condition as a slave.

Amendment XVI (Proposed 1909 – Ratified 1913)

Allows the government to tax income. [The federal government had to have a better and fairer source of income.]

Amendment XVII (Proposed 1912 – Ratified 1913)

United States Senators will be elected by the people directly rather than by state legislatures.
[The members of the Constitutional Convention feared direct election of senators by the people. Many people felt the Senate had become a rich man's club.]

Amendment XVIII (Proposed 1917 – Ratified 1919)

Forbids the making, selling, or shipping of intoxicating alcoholic products in the United States. [Alcohol abuse was the drug abuse of the time. Many people felt outlawing alcoholic beverages would solve the problem.]

Amendment XIX (Proposed 1919 – Ratified 1920)

Provides women the right to vote. [This was the result of an 80-year battle for women's suffrage.]

The Later Amendments (cont.)

Amendment XX (Proposed 1932 – Ratified 1933)

Reduces the time between the election of the president and the time his term begins which is now January 20 at 12:00 noon. It also specifies that the newly elected vice president becomes president if the president-elect dies before he could take office. It specifies the opening of the new term of Congress as January 3. [Travel time within the country had been reduced. Four months were no longer needed between election and beginning service.]

Amendment XXI (Proposed 1933 – Ratified 1933)

Repeals the 18th amendment and allows the making and sale of alcoholic beverages. [This experiment didn't work. It led to widespread abuse and organized crime.]

Amendment XXII (Proposed 1947 – Ratified 1951)

Limits the president to two terms or 10 years. If the vice president assumes the presidency with more than two years left in the term, he may only run for one term. [This was a response to Roosevelt's four election victories and fear of another popular president serving several terms.]

Amendment XXIII (Proposed 1960 – Ratified 1961)

The District of Columbia is given three electoral votes in the presidential election. [This was passed because citizens of the District of Columbia were denied a right to vote for president.]

Amendment XXIV (Proposed 1962 – Ratified 1964)

No person can be required to pay a tax in order to vote in any federal election for president, senators, or congressmen. [This prevented poll taxes which were used to limit African American voting in some Southern states.]

Amendment XXV (Proposed 1965 – Ratified 1967)

Specifies procedures for replacement of a president or vice president due to removal from office, death, or disability. It provides for the temporary replacement of the president by the vice president if the president requests it or the vice president and a majority of the cabinet believe the president cannot do his job. [In an age of nuclear weapons, the country could not afford a disabled or mentally disturbed president. The Cuban missile crisis and assassination of President Kennedy highlighted this need.]

Amendment XXVI (Proposed 1971 – Ratified 1971)

Reduces the voting age to 18 in all states. [With almost 10 years of Vietnam conflict, the feeling was that people old enough to die for their country were old enough to vote.]

Amendment XXVII (Proposed 1789 – Ratified 1992)

No change in the pay of senators or representatives can take effect until after the next congressional elections. [Originally proposed with the Bill of Rights, the 38th state ratified it in 1992.]

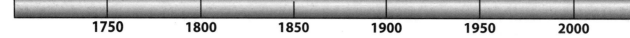

Unusual Facts About the Constitution

- Ben Franklin arrived at the State House in a Chinese sedan chair carried by four prisoners from a local jail. He was 81 and suffered from gout.

- Franklin suggested during the convention that if they had a long-term president who was bad, they might have to shoot him to get rid of him.

- Jared Ingersoll from the Pennsylvania delegation never once spoke during the meetings.

- Gouverneur Morris, who gave the most speeches during the convention (173), wrote the actual text of the Constitution in his own handwriting when the final document was being prepared.

- Two of the most important American leaders, Thomas Jefferson and John Adams, were in Europe during the convention. Both supported ratification.

- The 55 members of the convention kept their deliberations secret for four months even though members were always coming and going and several who were angry with the results left.

- The secrecy did lead to strange rumors being published. One rumor was that the members were going to select the second son of George III of Great Britain to be the king.

- Ben Franklin brought a two-headed snake to share.

- Alexander Hamilton had little use for states at all. He wanted the "United State of America."

- The Constitution does not specify a presidential cabinet of advisors. President Washington started the practice of consulting with the chiefs of each major department.

- Ben Franklin's last public act was to sign a memorial to Congress advocating the abolition of slavery.

- George Mason, a wealthy, aristocratic Virginia planter, was a strong advocate of democracy and clearly trusted the people to make good decisions. He also opposed the slave trade.

- Roger Sherman, a shoemaker's son from Connecticut, feared the people who were "too stupid and easily mislead."

- Rhode Island opposed even the idea of a convention and refused to send any delegate.

- New Hampshire's delegates arrived in late July because no money had been available.

- The longest period between amendments is 61 years, from 1804 to 1865—the period between the 12th and 13th Amendments.

- John Jay was appointed by President Washington as the first Chief Justice of the Supreme Court.

- There were three chief justices in the first 12 years. There were only two, John Marshall and Roger Taney, in the next 63 years.

- Only one man, William Howard Taft, has held both the offices of President of the United States and Chief Justice.

- One of the original 12 amendments proposed for the Bill of Rights in 1789 finally became law when it was ratified by the 38th state in 1992.

Reading Comprehension Quiz

The Constitution of the United States

Directions: Read pages 7–10 about the Constitution. Answer these questions based on the information in the selection. Circle the correct answer in each question below. Underline the sentence in the selection where the answer is found.

1. What portion of the slave population was counted for the purposes of representation in the House of Representatives?

   A one-half   C three-fifths

   B three-fourths   D one-third

2. How many senators are elected to represent each state?

   A three   C four

   B one   D two

3. Congress may not:

   A coin money   C declare war

   B grant a title of nobility   D collect taxes

4. Who is the executive head of government?

   A speaker   C president

   B chief justice   D senator

5. What fraction of all the states must approve an amendment before it becomes law?

   A one-third   C two-thirds

   B three-fifths   D three-fourths

6. How many states were needed to ratify the Constitution before it would take effect?

   A nine   C thirteen

   B eight   D fifty

7. What is treason?

   A voting in an election   C running for office

   B waging war on the U. S.   D coining money

8. How long is the term for a Supreme Court justice?

   A four years   C six years

   B for life   D fifteen years

9. Who is the Commander in Chief of the armed forces?

   A Congress   C Speaker of the House

   B the oldest senator   D President of the United States

10. Where must all bills for raising taxes originate?

    A House of Representatives   C Senate

    B Supreme Court   D president

Reading Comprehension Quiz

Creating the Constitution

Directions: Read pages 11–15 about the Articles of Confederation and the Constitutional Convention. Answer these questions based on the information in the selection. Circle the correct answer in each question below. Underline the sentence in the selection where the answer is found.

1. In which state did Shays' Rebellion occur?

   A Virginia   C New York

   B Massachusetts   D New Hampshire

2. Who created the Articles of Confederation?

   A Continental Congress   C President Washington

   B the Constitution   D Great Britain

3. Which of the following was true about the United States under the Articles of Confederation?

   A There was a strong navy.   C Paper money was valuable.

   B The U. S. owed no money.   D The U. S. owed many debts.

4. What was the largest number of delegates that attended the Constitutional Convention at any time?

   A 18   C 74

   B 55   D 39

5. In what year was the Constitutional Convention held?

   A 1789   C 1791

   B 1787   D 1786

6. Which two states refused to ratify the Constitution until a Bill of Rights was added?

   A Virginia and Delaware   C South Carolina and New Jersey

   B New York and Massachusetts D North Carolina and Rhode Island

7. How many states sent delegates to the Constitutional Convention at some time?

   A 50   C 9

   B 13   D 12

8. Which country would not allow American farmers to use the port of New Orleans?

   A Spain   C Great Britain

   B France   D United States

9. Where was the Constitutional Convention held?

   A Annapolis   C New York City

   B Boston   D Philadelphia

10. How much money did the national government under the Articles of Confederation owe altogether to foreign governments and on domestic loans?

   A 12 million dollars   C 25 million dollars

   B 52 million dollars   D 40 million dollars

Reading Comprehension Quiz

The Men at the Convention

Directions: Read pages 16–19 about The Convention Leaders. Answer these questions based on the information in the selection. Circle the correct answer in each question below. Underline the sentence in the selection where the answer is found.

1. Who is called the "Father of the Constitution"?
   - A   George Washington
   - B   James Madison
   - C   Ben Franklin
   - D   Gouverneur Morris

2. Which convention member had written "The Letters from a Farmer in Pennsylvania"?
   - A   Ben Franklin
   - B   Roger Sherman
   - C   Alexander Hamilton
   - D   John Dickinson

3. Which Connecticut signer of the Declaration of Independence feared democracy and felt the common people were stupid?
   - A   Roger Sherman
   - B   Elbridge Gerry
   - C   Edmund Randolph
   - D   Alexander Hamilton

4. Which New York delegate favored a powerful central government and a strong chief executive with almost king-like powers?
   - A   George Washington
   - B   Alexander Hamilton
   - C   Roger Sherman
   - D   Gouverneur Morris

5. Who was the presiding officer at the convention?
   - A   Thomas Jefferson
   - B   George Washington
   - C   James Madison
   - D   John Dickinson

6. Which delegate signed both the Declaration of Independence and the Articles of Confederation but not the Constitution?
   - A   Roger Sherman
   - B   George Washington
   - C   Elbridge Gerry
   - D   George Mason

7. Who wrote most of the Constitution in his own handwriting as a member of the Committee of Style and Arrangement?
   - A   Gouverneur Morris
   - B   James Madison
   - C   John Dickinson
   - D   Roger Sherman

8. Which New Yorker wrote at least 51 of The Federalist Papers in support of ratification?
   - A   James Madison
   - B   Alexander Hamilton
   - C   Roger Sherman
   - D   John Adams

9. Who had proposed the Albany Plan of Union in 1754?
   - A   George Washington
   - B   Benjamin Franklin
   - C   Roger Sherman
   - D   George Mason

10. Who kept extensive notes at the convention and devised the method of ratification?
    - A   John Adams
    - B   Governor Morris
    - C   James Madison
    - D   Edmund Randolph

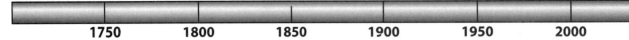
Reading Comprehension Quiz

Constitutional Compromises and Ratifying the Constitution

Directions: Read pages 20–24 about Constitutional Compromises and Ratifying the Constitution. Answer these questions based on the information in the selection. Circle the correct answer in each question below. Underline the sentence in the selection where the answer is found.

1. Which of the following was a feature of the Virginia Plan?
   - A two votes for each state
   - B one vote for each state
   - C all states must agree
   - D proportional representation

2. Why did the large states want voting in Congress to be based on population?
   - A they had more people
   - B they hated the smaller states
   - C they feared slavery
   - D to avoid war

3. Which compromise led to the establishment of a Congress with a Senate and a House of Representatives?
   - A the Virginia Plan
   - B the Connecticut Compromise
   - C Three-fifth's Compromise
   - D the New Jersey Compromise

4. Who deliberately stayed away from the convention during a crucial vote so that his colleague could cast Maryland's vote with the smaller states?
   - A George Washington
   - B Luther Martin
   - C Abraham Baldwin
   - D Daniel of St. Thomas Jenifer

5. What majority is required in Congress to override a presidential veto?
   - A two-thirds
   - B three-fifths
   - C three-fourths
   - D simple majority

6. Which part of government is designed to keep a check on the powers of both Congress and the presidency?
   - A the Supreme Court
   - B the army
   - C the Senate
   - D the state governors

7. How many states had to ratify the Constitution for it to take effect?
   - A 50
   - B 9
   - C 13
   - D 7

8. Which state was the first to ratify the Constitution?
   - A Virginia
   - B Delaware
   - C Pennsylvania
   - D New Jersey

9. Which Virginian did not support ratification?
   - A Patrick Henry
   - B Edmund Randolph
   - C George Mason
   - D John Marshall

10. Which two states were most critical to ratification?
    - A Delaware and Maryland
    - B Virginia and New York
    - C Massachusetts and Georgia
    - D New Jersey and Connecticut

Reading Comprehension Quiz

Supreme Court Decisions

Directions: Read pages 25 and 26. Use the information to match the letter of the Supreme Court Decision with the ruling which accompanied it.

A. *McCulloch v. Maryland*   D. *Brown v. Board of Education*
B. *Gibbons v. Ogden*   E. *Plessy v. Ferguson*
C. *Marbury v. Madison*   F. *Dred Scott Decision*

_____ desegregation of schools, restaurants, public facilities

_____ slaves are property and can't sue in court

_____ Congress has "implied powers" not stated in Constitution

_____ Supreme Court has right to judicial review of laws

_____ states may not interfere in interstate commerce

_____ "separate but equal" facilities allowed for African Americans

Amendment Match

Directions: Read pages 27–29. Use the information to match the number of the amendment with the provisions listed below. The first one is done for you. Some numbers are used more than once.

_____8_____ no excessive bail or cruel and unusual punishments

_____ a person is entitled to a fair, speedy, public trial

_____ some powers are reserved to the states and the people

_____ women have the right to vote

_____ people have the right to a free press

_____ slavery is forbidden in the United States

_____ no one can be prevented from voting because of race

_____ voting age is 18

_____ people have the right to assemble peaceably

_____ no taxes on voting are permitted

_____ people have the right to own and carry firearms

_____ a person cannot be forced to testify against himself

_____ prohibition on the sale and production of alcohol

_____ repeal on the prohibition of alcohol

_____ a person's property may not be searched without a warrant

_____ Congress may not establish any religion

_____ a jury trial is permitted in civil suits over $20 in value

_____ people have the right to free speech

_____ a person has the right to a lawyer in a criminal case

_____ a suspect has the right to know the charges against him

_____ U. S. Senators will be directly elected by the people

_____ allows the use of taxes on income

_____ limits the President to two terms or 10 years service

_____ the District of Columbia receives three electoral votes

Teacher Lesson Plans

Geography — Working with Maps

Objective: Students will learn to use and derive information from a variety of map forms.

Materials

- copies of The 13 Original States (page 37)
- copies of The United States Today (page 38)
- atlases, almanacs, and other maps for reference and comparison

Procedure

1. Review The 13 Original States activity page. Review the map on the page. Have the students use the information on pages 22–24 and other suggested resources to complete the page.
2. Review The United States Today map (page 38). Have the students answer the questions at the bottom of the page.

Assessment—Correct the activity pages with the students. Check for understanding and review basic concepts.

• •

Written Language and Oral Language

Objective: Students will develop skills in persuasive writing and oral presentation techniques in speech and debate.

Materials

- copies of Keeping a Journal (page 39)
- copies of Take a Stand (pages 41 and 42)
- copies of Public Speaking (page 44)
- books, encyclopedias, and Internet sources
- copies of Writing Laws (page 40)
- copies of Giving a Speech (page 43)
- copies of Great Debates (page 45)

Procedures

1. Review the format students should use for journal writing (date, first person, etc.). Distribute Keeping a Journal (page 39) and review the prompts with the students. Encourage the students to complete all of the activities.
2. Distribute Writing Laws (page 40) with the students. Review the importance of laws in all communities. Encourage students to do all the activities.
3. Distribute Take a Stand (pages 41 and 42). Review the format for a persuasive essay. Allow students ample time to complete the essay using the writing process.
4. Distribute Giving a Speech (page 43) and Public Speaking (page 44). Allow each student to choose a favorite topic. Schedule time for students to write and deliver their speeches. Encourage students to select a famous speech or a portion of the speech to deliver.
5. Distribute Great Debates (page 45). Review the debating process and the need to be serious and courteous when debating opponents. Assign students to the debate panels.

Assessment—Have students share stories, speeches, and debates with the entire class. Encourage all students to critique their activities.

The 13 Original States

1. Creat a chart like the one below. List the 13 original states. List the month and year they ratified the Constitution. Refer to a copy of the Constitution (Article I) to determine how many senators and how many representatives each state had.

State	Date Admitted Month/Year	Number of Representatives	Number of Senators

2. Name the three largest states: _____

3. Name the two smallest states: _____

4. Why did New York's location make it so important that it ratify the Constitution?

_____

_____

The United States Today

The members of the Constitutional Convention were very concerned about the size of individual states, especially in terms of their population. Population affected both membership in Congress and the Electoral College which casts votes for the president. The people of a state cast votes for a slate of electors committed to a particular candidate. The number of electoral votes in a state is equal to the number of senators (2) plus the number of representatives in a state. (The District of Columbia is not a state. It has 3 electoral votes but no senators or representatives.)

This map shows the number of electoral votes in each state. Study the map above and answer these questions.

1. Which state has the most electoral votes?_____

2. Which states have only 3 electoral votes—the fewest any state can have? _____

   _____

3. It takes 270 electoral votes to elect a president. What is the fewest number of states it would take
   to elect a president?_____ List the states._____

   _____

4. Which states have only two members of the House of Representatives?_____

5. How many electoral votes does your state have? _____

6. How many members of the House of Representatives does you state have? _____

| 1750 | 1800 | 1850 | 1900 | 1950 | 2000 |

Keeping a Journal

Many of the Founding Fathers who wrote the Constitution and other documents of American liberty were men who kept diaries and journals throughout their lives. James Madison kept very detailed notes of the proceedings at the Constitutional Convention and much of our knowledge about the convention comes from his writing.

A Day in the Life of. . .You

Directions: Keep a journal of your daily activities for one 24-hour period. Include as many of the following activities as you can.

- when and what you ate—meals and snacks
- bedtime and sleep
- what you learned and did in each class at school
- books and other reading material

- games and sports you played at recess and at home
- computer usage
- homework
- television
- ideas, thoughts, opinions, plans, and other creative activity

Assessment—What was good, bad, or special about your day? Write a short essay to describe your day.

History Journal – This Week in the World

Watch or listen to at least one daily newscast. Keep a journal for one week recording the news events that happen in your nation, in the world, and in your life. Some of these topics would include:

- wars or battles
- natural disasters
- science and medical news
- school news

- presidential actions
- deaths
- strange and unexplained happenings
- personal events in your life

Two-Week Math Journal

Math is a subject in which most students are taught a new concept almost every day. Keeping a daily record of your math activities can make you a much better student and make the subject much more useful and understandable. Use a separate page each day to record the math idea or ideas of the day and sample problems.

Science or Pet Diary

The best science students study a subject over an extended period of time and keep daily records of what they have learned. You could do this project by studying a pet hamster, mouse, rat, bird, cat, dog, or even insects. You might also choose a wild creature or a plant. Record information about the animal's behavior, feeding habits, sleeping time, housekeeping activities, and any observations or impressions you make.

Writing Laws

Writing laws that everyone can live with is a very difficult assignment as the Founding Fathers at the Constitutional Convention knew. They needed to know how to compromise effectively. They had to respect the opinions of others with whom they disagreed and they had to decide when a principle was too important to give up. They also had to design a method to get approval for their document and to devise ways the Constitution could be changed. The document they produced has lasted more than 225 years.

Class Rules

In a committee of three or four students, write a list of rules which should be followed by everyone in the class. Keep the following notes in mind:

Playground Rules

- Each rule should be short and easy to understand.
- Your group members should agree to accept all of the rules, even if one member doesn't like a specific rule.
- Reasonable consequences should follow if a rule is broken.
- The group should decide who will impose the punishments for rule-breaking.
- The rules cannot discriminate against any classmate on the basis of race, gender, religion, or appearance.
- The rules should be clearly posted on a chart.
- There should be no more than seven rules.

In a committee of three or four students, try to formulate a set of playground rules which all students should follow. Remember to keep the conditions mentioned above in mind. You will also want to consider these:

Issues in the 21st Century

- special needs for smaller and younger children
- safe places for students with physical disabilities to play
- safety concerns, especially in softball, football, and soccer
- activities which are forbidden or dangerous
- playground language, arguments, and ways to settle disputes

The men at the convention were forced to compromise on issues which divided their countrymen. These included conflicts between large and small states, disputes between farmers and city dwellers, Northern and Southern state interests, those for and against slavery, those who favored strong government and those who favored weak government, rich versus poor, conflicts between religious believers, frontier communities versus more settled areas, and many other political differences.

1. Make a list of at least 10 issues on which Americans hold divided opinions today. Use media sources such as radio, magazines, newspapers, television, and the Internet to help you.

2. On a chart, prioritize your list so that the most important issue is number 1 and the least important is number 10. Compare your list with your classmates' lists.

Take a Stand

Throughout American history, American citizens have heatedly discussed and debated the great issues of their times. They often published letters and essays in newspapers and magazines expressing their views.

Persuasive Essay

Write a persuasive essay on one of the suggested topics listed below or another subject about which you have strong opinions.

Your essay should have at least four paragraphs like this:

1. An opening paragraph should clearly express your opinion and indicate why the subject is important to you.
2. The second paragraph should describe all of the evidence you can think of to support your opinion—this could include personal experiences, the opinions of experts, and careful reasoning.
3. The third paragraph should describe the arguments and evidence against your position and your response and reactions to these arguments.
4. The concluding paragraph should briefly restate your position and clearly draw together all the elements of your thinking.

Suggested Topics

- Should uniforms be required in school?

- Should the driving age be lowered to 14?

- The greatest invention in the world was _____ .

- Girls and boys should attend separate classes.

- Should the United States have gone to war in Vietnam?

- Should the United States have gone to war in Iraq?

- The greatest American president was _____ .

- Should the President of the United States have to have a Declaration of War from Congress before sending troops into any conflict?

- Should some students receive preferential admissions to colleges because they come from disadvantaged communities?

- Science is more important than art.

- The most important subject in school is _____ .

- Grades should be abolished in schools.

- The best book ever written is _____ .

- Should the atomic bomb have been used to end World War II?

- The best sport is _____ .

Take a Stand *(cont.)*

Pre-write

Do your pre-write planning or cluster here.

Title: _____

_____

_____

your opinion/importance of the subject	arguments against your position and your response
the evidence and your experiences	**concluding statement**

Giving a Speech

Many of the men who wrote the Constitution were distinguished public speakers. They had often been involved in speaking against British control of the colonies. They spoke regularly as members of their state legislatures, the Continental Congress, or Congress under the Articles of Confederation. James Madison spoke at the Constitutional Convention on 161 occasions. Gouverneur Morris addressed the delegates 173 times. James Wilson of Pennsylvania spoke 168 times. Some delegates were not admired for their speaking abilities. Luther Martin never seemed to stop, but he often put Ben Franklin to sleep. Roger Sherman was often hard to understand. On the other hand, Jared Ingersoll of Pennsylvania never said a word.

Write a Speech

Choose a topic which interests you. Choose one of the topics on the next page or another subject. Write a speech about three minutes long to deliver to your class. Your speech should have:

- an opening paragraph stating your purpose
- two to four paragraphs expressing each of the main points in clear, logical, precise language
- a concluding paragraph which summarizes your thinking

Refine Your Speech

Your speech will have a greater effect on your listeners if you use:

- anecdotes or stories to illustrate some of your main points
- evidence and facts to support each of your main points
- one or two brief quotations from experts to support your opinions
- an attention-getting opening sentence
- a sharply focused closing sentence

Delivering Your Speech

You may choose to memorize your speech and simply use your paper as a crutch if you forget something. Another method is to use note cards and speak extemporaneously, in an impromptu manner, as if you were speaking to friends. In either style of speech, use these techniques to connect with your audience.

Good Posture – Stand straight. Balance your feet. Relax your body. Tell yourself to be comfortable. Center your mind.

Eye Contact – Look at various sections of the audience as you speak but not at any one person in particular.

Rehearse Out Loud – Give your speech out loud in full voice to a mirror, a friend, a younger sibling, or your parents. Practice several times.

Volume – Vary your voice pattern. Be conversational at some times. Speak more forcefully on important points. Never shout but always be loud enough to be heard.

Breathe from Your Diaphragm – Take deep breaths between paragraphs and important points but don't be obvious about it. (The diaphragm is the large muscle at the bottom of your rib cage which allows you to control your breathing.)

Speak Slowly and Clearly – Speak a little slower than you do in your normal speech pattern. Don't race to get done.

Enjoy the Experience – Public speaking is a great accomplishment.

Public Speaking

Topics

Below are a few topics to consider for your speech. Feel free to change the topic or use one of your own.

- ❏ My Favorite _____
- ❏ War
- ❏ The Greatest American
- ❏ How to Diaper a Baby
- ❏ Being a Parent
- ❏ Living Left-handed
- ❏ My Favorite (or Least Favorite) Subject
- ❏ Cats and Dogs
- ❏ The Best President
- ❏ Television
- ❏ How to Throw a Football
- ❏ Animals Have Feelings Too

- ❏ A Wonderful Day
- ❏ Drug Abuse
- ❏ Homework
- ❏ How to Pitch a Baseball
- ❏ The Best Book Ever Written
- ❏ My Little Sister (or Brother)
- ❏ Animal Experimentation
- ❏ Atomic Weapons
- ❏ My Hero
- ❏ How to Play Video Games
- ❏ My Favorite Teacher
- ❏ Poverty

Great Speeches

One kind of public speaking involves memorizing all or part of a great speech by a famous person and delivering it to an audience. Sometimes parts of famous documents like the Preamble to the Constitution or the Introduction to the Declaration of Independence are used. Speakers may also choose a long speech in a play, called a *soliloquy*. Certain special parts of a book might also be used.

Assignment

Choose one of the suggested speeches listed below. Select a part of the speech or the entire speech if it is less than five minutes long. Memorize the speech. Try to get the tone and emphasis that the original speaker might have used. Deliver your speech to the class.

Selections

You can find these on the Internet, in books of famous speeches, in encyclopedias, in books about the speaker, and other sources.

- The Gettysburg Address by Abraham Lincoln
- President Kennedy's Inaugural Address
- "I Have A Dream" by Martin Luther King Jr.
- Franklin D. Roosevelt's First Inaugural Address
- Winston Churchill's Iron Curtain Speech
- Abraham Lincoln's Second Inaugural Address
- The Preamble and Declaration of Rights in The Declaration of Independence
- Hamlet's "To Be or Not to Be" Soliloquy

- Daniel Webster's Bunker Hill Oration
- Benjamin Franklin's Final Speech at the Convention
- Ronald Reagan's Challenger Disaster Speech
- Patrick Henry's "Give Me Liberty or Give Me Death" Oration
- Sojourner Truth's "Ain't I a Woman?"
- Seneca Falls Convention's Declaration of the Rights of Women
- "All the World's a Stage" from Shakespeare's *As You Like It*

Great Debates

The Constitutional Convention was the scene of many speeches and debates among the delegates. Men like James Madison, Roger Sherman, Alexander Hamilton, and Benjamin Franklin were widely respected for their ability to respond to an argument or present an intelligent and coherent plan.

Debate Format

Formal debates usually are phrased like the following example:

> **Resolved:** That no person should be allowed to serve more than 12 years in Congress.

Debate topics are usually written about subjects which are clearly open to much discussion, about which there is a great deal of evidence on both sides of the issue, and which are important to people as citizens of their country.

The affirmative side on a debate panel argues that the resolution is correct. In the example above, the affirmative side would argue that Congressmen would have to leave office after 12 years which would be two Senate terms or six terms in the House of Representatives.

The negative side of a debate panel would argue that the resolution was not good policy. In this case, they would argue for unrestricted service in the Senate or the House.

Your Debate

You and your team will choose a topic such as those described on page 44. You will need to write the topic in the correct format as shown above.

Resolved That. . . _____

_____

_____

_____

You will have four members of your debate panel divided into two teams. You will be assigned to debate either the affirmative or the negative viewpoint of your topic. It is not important that you agree with the viewpoint you are debating. It is important to learn how to take a position and defend it using all of the facts and evidence you can collect and to be able to organize it into effective talking points.

A constructive speech lists all the evidence and arguments in favor of the position you are debating—affirmative or negative.

A rebuttal is a response to arguments made by the other side.

Debate Format

Speeches will be given in the following order.

1. First constructive speech by affirmative team. (4 minutes)*
2. First constructive speech by negative team. (4 minutes)
3. First rebuttal by negative team. (2 minutes)
4. First rebuttal by affirmative team. (2 minutes)
5. Second rebuttal by negative team. (1 minute)
6. Second rebuttal by affirmative team. (1 minute)

*Time limits are strictly enforced.

*Team members may share the time.

*Team members need to organize their evidence and discuss tactics with each other.

*Team members should practice their speeches with each other.

Teacher Lesson Plans

Working with Timelines

Objectives: Students will learn to derive information from a timeline and make timelines relevant to them.

Materials

- copies of Constitution Timeline/United States History (pages 47 and 48)
- research resources including books, encyclopedias, texts, atlases, almanacs, and Internet sites

Procedure

1. Collect all available resources for your students so that they have plenty of places to find information.

2. Reproduce and distribute the Constitution Timeline/United States History (pages 47 and 48) activity sheet. Review the concept of a timeline, possibly using the school year as an example.

3. Review the various events listed on the timeline.

4. Assign students to find additional dates for the timeline as described in the assignment on page 48.

5. Students may want to use the readings from previous lessons to locate additional dates for their timelines.

6. Have students create their own personal timelines as described in the assignment at the bottom of page 48.

Assessment—Share additions to timeline in classroom discussion using a board or chart to list the new dates. Have students share their personal timelines in small groups.

• •

Famous People Research

Objectives: Students will develop skills in finding, organizing, and presenting research information.

Materials

- copies of Become a Famous Person (pages 49–52)
- copies of Famous People of the Era (page 53)
- books, encyclopedias, and Internet sources

Procedure

1. Review the information shared on the Become a Famous Person activity (pages 49–52). Stress organizing material, studying notes, and techniques for presentation. Then, review the research guidelines.

2. Review list of potential famous people on the Famous People of the Era (page 53) sheet. Solicit other suggestions and add them to the sheet.

3. Review information on becoming a famous person. Review research guidelines.

4. Allow students time to prepare their research-based presentations. Then, arrange a schedule of presentations.

Assessment—Assess students on the basis of their written notes and oral classroom presentations.

Constitution Timeline/United States History

1775	The first battles of the American Revolution occur at Lexington and Concord on April 19.
1776	The Declaration of Independence is proclaimed.
1777	The Articles of Confederation are adopted by the Continental Congress.
1781	British General Cornwallis surrenders to Washington at Yorktown bringing an end to the Revolutionary War.
1783	The Treaty of Paris formally ends the American Revolution.
1784	A major depression injures U. S. economy, making problems of debt repayment more difficult.
1786	A new coinage system based on the decimal system is enacted by Congress under the Articles of Confederation.
1787	Shays' Rebellion, a farmers' uprising caused by debt and land foreclosure, is put down by the Massachusetts militia.
1787	The Constitutional Convention meets in Philadelphia from May to September.
1787	Delaware, Pennsylvania, and New Jersey ratify the Constitution in December.
1788	Georgia, Connecticut, Massachusetts, Maryland, South Carolina, New Hampshire, Virginia, and New York ratify the Constitution.
1789	In April the first Congress is organized and George Washington is inaugurated as president.
1789	North Carolina ratifies the Constitution in November.
1790	Rhode Island becomes the 13th state to ratify the Constitution.
1791	The Bill of Rights, the first 10 amendments to the Constitution, becomes law.
1798	The 11th amendment limits federal jurisdiction over individuals of one state suing another state.
1801	John Marshall, whose leadership helps make the Court an equal branch of government, is appointed Chief Justice of the Supreme Court.
1803	The United States purchases the Louisiana Territory from France.
1804	The Lewis and Clark Expedition begins its two-year journey of exploration from the Mississippi to the Pacific Ocean.
1804	The 12th amendment provides for separate ballots for president and vice president.
1814	Washington, D.C., is captured by the British during the War of 1812, and the White House and Capitol are set afire.
1836	The battle of the Alamo is fought. Texas achieves its independence from Mexico.
1848	The California gold rush begins.
1860	Abraham Lincoln is elected president.
1861	The Civil War commences with the firing on Fort Sumter.
1865	The Civil War ends and Lincoln is assassinated.
1865	The 13th Amendment abolishes slavery.
1868	The 14th Amendment grants citizenship to former slaves.
1868	Andrew Johnson is the first president to be impeached.
1869	The 15th Amendment grants African Americans the right to vote.

Constitution Timeline/ United States History *(cont.)*

1906	Massive earthquake rocks San Francisco.
1913	The 16th Amendment authorizes an income tax.
1913	The 17th Amendment provides for the direct election of U. S. Senators.
1917	The United States enters World War I.
1918	World War I ends.
1920	The 19th Amendment grants women the right to vote.
1933	The 20th Amendment makes slight adjustments in the terms of the president, vice president, senators, and representatives.
1933	The 21st Amendment repeals the 18th Amendment.
1941	Japan's attack on Pearl Harbor brings the United States into World War II.
1945	The surrender of Germany and Japan ends World War II.
1951	The 22nd Amendment limits the president to two terms.
1954	The Supreme Court outlaws segregation in public schools.
1961	The 23rd Amendment grants citizens in the District of Columbia the right to vote in presidential elections.
1964	The 24th Amendment bars poll taxes in federal elections.
1967	The 25th Amendment provides for succession to the presidency (as a result) of death, resignation, or disability.
1971	The 26th Amendment lowers the voting age to 18.
1974	Watergate scandal leads to the resignation of President Nixon.
1992	The 27th Amendment affecting Congressional pay increases is ratified.
1998	Personal scandal leads to President Clinton's impeachment.
2003	The United States engages in a war with Iraq.

Assignment

1. Study the timeline above.

2. Find at least 10 dates in American history to add to the timeline. They may go before, during, or after the timeline. These dates could include wars, inventions, presidential elections, disasters, or sporting events among many other occasions. Make a list of these dates in chronological (time) order to share with the class. Be sure you know a little background information about each of your additional dates.

3. Make a month-by-month timeline of the progress of the Constitution from the first meetings of the convention in May 1787 to the ratification by New York in July 1788.

4. Create a timeline of your personal lifetime since the year you were born. Include the important events of your life. Then add events that happened in your country or the world during the same time. These events could include terrorist attacks, wars, presidential elections, important people who died, sporting events, earthquakes, floods, or happenings in popular culture.

Become a Famous Person

A great way to really understand history is to become an important historical character. You will become familiar not only with the person but the times in which he or she lived. You will understand the issues of the day and acquire a sense of the day-to-day lifestyle of your famous person.

Select a Person

Choose a member of the Constitutional Convention or another person from the list on page 53 or choose anyone from the late 1700s or early 1800s who had an impact on American history. Read enough about the individual to make sure that it is someone who interests you and who will hold your attention. Before you finalize your choice, make sure that you can find several books in the library about your person as well as Internet Websites.

Because so many of the famous people from this time period are male, some girls may feel comfortable adopting a male Founding Father or other public leader. This will be made somewhat easier because many of the men of that time wore long hair. The list on page 53 also includes women who had an impact on the times.

Do the Research

Use the research model on the next two pages to find out everything you can about your person. Know the important dates, the vital statistics, the personal life, and the struggles of your famous person. Become familiar with your person's accomplishments. Begin to think of yourself as that person. Try to assume the attitude and the personality of your person.

Go to the Sources

- Use encyclopedias, almanacs, biographies, the Internet, and other sources of information to acquire the basic facts you need.
- You should find and use at least two full-length biographies about your person. You can also use adult biographies to research material not available in children's books.
- Use the Index and Table of Contents of an adult biography to target specific information you need to know more about.

Take Careful Notes

- Use your own words.
- Write your facts clearly and briefly.
- Write down the basic facts in an orderly way. (The outline on pages 51 and 52 shows one good format to use.)
- Look for anecdotes and funny stories about your person.
- Study the notes.
- Get a friend to quiz you about your person so that you know what you need to study and are confident about what you know.
- When other students are being questioned, write down questions you couldn't answer about your own person and look the answers up later.

Become a Famous Person *(cont.)*

Get in Costume

- Put together an appropriate costume. Check your closets at home for pants, slacks, shirts, or old costumes which might work. Check with parents, grandparents, older siblings, and friends for articles of clothing that might help. Ask for help getting to thrift stores for the missing pieces.
- Find a wig and comb it to the right shape or use cotton balls glued to a swimming cap or nylon stocking for a white wig.
- Use a period hat instead of a wig if you like. Hats can often be shaped from dark construction paper or tagboard.

Footwear and Props

- Don't wear tennis shoes. (They weren't invented yet.) Use or borrow moccasin-like bedroom slippers, leather boots, or leather shoes. If they're too big, stuff them with tissue before putting them on for your presentation.
- Try to use a prop that fits with your character. A sword for Washington, a journal for Madison, or a kite for Franklin, are some examples of effective props.

Be Famous

"My name is _____ . What would you like to know about me?"

This is one way to begin your presentation. You might also want to give a brief presentation listing five or six important facts about your famous person. This will give your classmates a place to begin with their questions. Have a story to tell or something else to say if there is a momentary lull in the questioning.

Stay in Character

Don't forget who you are. You are a famous person—not another student in the class. Be very serious. Avoid any silly behaviors. At the end of the questions, review the important facts about your life.

Be Dramatic

- Use a loud voice. Don't drop your voice at the end of sentences.
- Use gestures. Use your arms and prop to emphasize your points.
- Take charge of the classroom. Stride across the front.
- Be forceful, assertive, and self-assured.
- Have faith in yourself.

Become a Famous Person *(cont.)*

Directions: Use these guidelines to help you find important information about your famous person.

Research Guidelines

I. Youth

  A. Birthplace and date

  B. Home life and experiences
- 1. siblings (brothers and sisters)
- 2. places lived (parts of the country) (farm or town)
- 3. circumstances (rich or poor) (important events to you)
- 4. age when you left home
- 5. parents (names and a fact or two)
- 6. activities and hobbies during childhood

  C. Schooling (When?) (How much?)

  D. Childhood heroes

  E. Interesting facts and stories about your youth

II. Adult Life

  A. Adventures and experiences
- 1. give details of each adventure or experience
- 2. places you traveled to
- 3. fights and wars
- 4. dangers you faced
- 5. friends and companions in your adventures

  B. Lifestyle and personal habits
- 1. personal attitude toward life (list examples)
- 2. values you believe in
- 3. were you a risk-taker or cautious? (give examples)
- 4. personal behavior (cruel, kind, honest, etc.)
- 5. leadership experiences (Did men follow you? Why?)
- 6. physical abilities and disabilities (illnesses, physical problems)

  C. Personal information
- 1. marriage/children
- 2. jobs held
- 3. adult hobbies and interests

  D. Reasons for fame
- 1. firsts (anything you accomplished first in human history)
- 2. inventions and discoveries (give complete details)
- 3. contributions to the human race or destructive acts (give details and reasons you did what you did)
- 4. accomplishments (name and describe successes)
- 5. failures and things you didn't complete
- 6. greatest challenges you faced (describe and explain)
- 7. impact on United States or the world (importance of what you did)

Become a Famous Person (cont.)

Research Guidelines (cont.)

II. **Adult Life** (cont.)

    E. Your role in writing the Constitution (if you were involved)

        1. state you represented

        2. your attitudes and opinions about the document

        3. problems you faced at the Constitutional Convention

        4. other people who agreed with you

        5. adversaries (opponents) at the Constitutional Convention

        6. your role in ratification

III. **End of Life**

    A. Death

        1. date of death

        2. age when you died

        3. cause of death (facts about the death)

        4. other facts about your death

        5. last words spoken (if known)

        6. epitaph (words on tombstone, if any)

    B. Fame

        1. Were you famous at the time of death?

        2. Were you admired or forgotten by the time of your death?

IV. **The Life and Times**

    A. Contemporaries

        1. other famous people alive during your lifetime

        2. presidents and public leaders of the time

    B. Inventions and discoveries

        1. important inventions of the time period

        2. discoveries in medicine, science, or exploration

    C. Travel and transportation

        1. how people traveled (boats, horses, other means)

        2. how goods and products were moved

    D. Important events

        1. wars and conflicts of the time

        2. disasters (earthquakes, depressions, crashes, etc.)

V. **Personal Evaluation**

    A. Admirable qualities

    B. Unpleasant behaviors and prejudices

    C. How you feel about your person

    D. Questions you would ask your person if you could

    E. Would you trust this person in your home? (reasons)

Famous People of the Era

Here are some of the Constitutional Convention leaders and several other people of interest and importance from 1760 through 1820.

Convention Leaders

James Madison – "Father of the Constitution"

George Washington – presiding officer at the Constitutional Convention

Benjamin Franklin – delegate from Pennsylvania

Alexander Hamilton – proponent of strong national government

Edmund Randolph – presented the Virginia Plan

Gouverneur Morris – his handwriting is on the document

George Mason – proponent of a Bill of Rights

John Dickinson – revolutionary activist; Delaware delegate

Roger Sherman – distrusted the common people

Elbridge Gerry – feared democracy but wanted Bill of Rights

Less Well-known Convention Delegates

Jonathan Dayton – youngest delegate

William Paterson – opposed the Virginia Plan

James Wilson – strong supporter of national government

Luther Martin – favored small states and weak national government

Rufus King – important Massachusetts delegate

Robert Morris – financial expert

Other Important Public Figures

John Adams – ambassador to England; revolutionary war leader

Thomas Jefferson – ambassador, president, inventor

Patrick Henry – he "smelled a rat"

John Marshall – future leader of Supreme Court

John Jay – helped write The Federalist Papers

Daniel Shays – led a rebellion in Massachusetts

Thomas Paine – author of *Common Sense*

Samuel Adams – leader of the Sons of Liberty

John Hancock – signer of the Declaration of Independence

Heroes, Heroines, Explorers, Inventors, Creators

Joseph Brant – Mohawk Indian war leader

Mercy Otis Warren – dramatist, historian, revolutionary

Abigail Adams – advocate for women

Deborah Sampson – female soldier in Revolutionary War

Richard Henry Lee – war hero

Lydia Darragh – spy for Washington's army

Benjamin Banneker – African-American inventor, scientist

Emma Willard – founded first female academy

Phillis Wheatley – African-American poet

Meriwether Lewis – co-captain of the great expedition

William Clark – co-captain of the great expedition

Sacagawea – Shoshone interpreter and guide

Davy Crockett – famous explorer, frontiersman, Congressman

Mary Jemison – white leader in Seneca tribe

Daniel Boone – famous explorer who opened Kentucky territory

John Chapman – frontier hero and tree planter

Benjamin Rush – foremost American medical scientist

Sequoya – developed first written Indian language

Sarah Josepha Hale – first female magazine editor

Betty Zane – border heroine who saved Fort Henry

Andrew Jackson – war hero; first frontier president

Teacher Lesson Plans

Readers Theater

Objective: Students will learn to use their voices effectively in dramatic reading.

Materials

- copies of Readers Theater (pages 55–57)
- various sources about the Constitution

Procedure

1. Review basic concept of Readers Theater with class. The Readers Theater will help you to stress the important skills.

2. Have students read over the Readers Theater (pages 55–57). Place students in small groups and allow time to practice reading the script over several days.

3. Schedule class performances and have students share the prepared script.

4. Then, use the suggestions on the bottom of page 55 to assign topics to teams of students. Allow student teams time to create and practice their scripts.

5. Schedule classroom performances of these scripts.

Assessment—Base performance assessments on pacing, volume, expression, and focus of the participants. Student-created scripts should demonstrate general writing skills, dramatic tension, and a good plot.

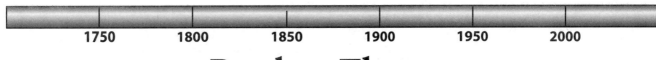

Readers Theater

Readers Theater is drama without costumes, props, stage, or memorization. It is done in the classroom by groups of students who become the cast of the dramatic reading.

Staging

Your classroom is the stage. Place four or five stools or chairs in a semicircle at the front of your class or in a separate staging area. You may use simple costumes but generally no costume is expected or used in this type of dramatization. If you have plain robes or simple coats of the same color or style so that everyone looks about the same, this can have a nice effect. Students dressed in the same school uniform or colors create an atmosphere of seriousness. Props are not needed, but they may be used for additional details.

Scripting

Each member of your group should have a clearly marked, useable script. You will have a chance to practice several times before presenting to the class.

Performing

You should enter quietly and seriously into the classroom. Sit silently and unmoving on the stools or chairs and wait with heads lowered or focus on a point above the audience. The narrator should start reading and the actors will then focus on their scripts. The actors should focus on whoever is reading, except when they are performing.

Extensions

Feel free to add movement and memorization to the performances. You can introduce mime to the performance and add props or costumes, as the circumstances allow. Some actors may begin to add accents as they become more familiar with the format.

Assignment

1. Read the script (pages 56 and 57) about the Constitutional Convention. Work within your group to prepare for the performance and share your interpretation of the script with the class.

2. Next, you get an opportunity to write and perform your own Readers Theater script. Write a script based on one of these events or another one related to the Constitutional Convention. Use some of the books listed in the bibliography on page 61 as sources of ideas.

    • The Virginia Plan is introduced to the convention.

    • The New Jersey Plan is debated.

    • The final signing day at the convention

    • Patrick Henry "smells a rat" and refuses to attend the convention.

    • A hot day in the State House as members quarrel and the temperature rises

    • Ratification in Virginia or New York

    • The debates over slavery

3. After practicing your script, share your performance with the rest of the class.

Readers Theater *(cont.)*

Script

This script is an abbreviated account of the discussions at the Constitutional Convention relating to the nature of the presidency which the Founding Fathers were creating. There are seven speaking parts.

Narrator: The delegates to the Constitutional Convention were deeply divided over who should lead the new government they were creating. Some delegates, like Alexander Hamilton, wanted a president to serve for many years or even a lifetime, like a king. Others wanted the office to have little real power and the term to be only one or two years.

Edmund Randolph: What we need to create, gentlemen, is a strong national government with a Congress to make laws, a president to enforce those laws, and a judicial branch to determine that they are fair and equitable. Our poor nation right now is a collection of weak and arguing states who don't trust each other. They impose taxes on each other and sometimes are even at the point of war.

John Dickinson: We just got rid of one king. I'll not have another one. Keep the states as they are.

Elbridge Gerry: We were sent here to revise the Articles of Confederation—not to form a nation with a king or some other powerful leader.

Alexander Hamilton: This country needs strong leadership—otherwise it is going to be gobbled up by European empires. What we need is a president for life.

John Dickinson: No, I don't agree. A president with very little power is what we desire. The weaker he is the safer we will be. One year is long enough for any president.

James Madison: He has to be strong or this nation will blow away like leaves in the wind with every state going broke, being swallowed up by other countries, or always getting into wars.

Elbridge Gerry: I don't trust any ruler. All he'll want to do is raise taxes and get us into war. He will end up a king with a different title.

James Madison: This country needs leadership. We cannot afford to have a weak or feeble chief executive. He must be able to act with force when necessary.

Readers Theater *(cont.)*

Script *(cont.)*

Narrator: Many delegates were fearful that the presidency would pass from father to son like a monarchy, or that the president would rule the country without regard to the Congress or the rule of law.

Elbridge Gerry: Why does it have to be a president for life—why not six years or four or one year?

Alexander Hamilton: Well, it would be embarrassing to have a lot of ex-presidents wandering around like ghosts with nothing much to do.

Benjamin Franklin: But suppose you had a lifetime president or even one with a six year term and he turned out to be a worthless president. What could you do about it? We might have to arrange some way to get rid of a president who is incompetent or sick or who commits a crime. Otherwise, we might have to shoot him.

Narrator: Many of the delegates were amused by Ben Franklin's suggestion but they also recognized the problem. What would ex-presidents do? Would they go back home to their businesses and farms or would they find other jobs in government? The delegates were also uncertain about what to call the leader of this new office they were creating.

Elbridge Gerry: How will we address this president?

Alexander Hamilton: I think that he should be called His Highness or His Excellency.

Elbridge Gerry: Sounds just like a king to me or some other high-fallutin' gentry.

Benjamin Franklin: How about just plain, Mister, such as Mr. Randolph or Mr. Madison?

Elbridge Gerry: How about Mr. President? It's simple, dignified, and it doesn't put on airs.

John Dickinson: That sounds just right.

Culminating Activities

Constitutional Convention Day

Set aside one day to be devoted to activities related to your study of the Constitution of the United States. If possible, do this activity with two or three classes at the same grade level. This allows you to share some of the burdens and provides a special experience for the entire grade level.

Costumes

Encourage all of your students to come in period costumes. Most students could use their famous people costumes. Others would find period clothes with a look of the colonial or early national period. As with the famous people project, ask children to find leather shoes, boots, or moccasins and avoid tennis shoes which are very modern in concept. Ask one or two mothers to use makeup to provide some mustaches and beards to give a period look to the day.

Parent Help

Encourage as many parents or older siblings as you can to come for all or part of the day to enjoy the proceedings and to help set up and monitor the activities. This is truly a day involving the family in the educational process. It helps to survey parents to discover any special talents, interests, or hobbies that would be a match for specific centers.

Doing Centers

- The centers you set up should relate in some way to the Constitutional Convention or daily life during that time.

- Centers should involve the children in an activity and often in making something they can take or put on display.

- The class should be divided into groups with about six or seven students in each group.

- Each center should take about 20 to 30 minutes. Students then rotate to the next activity.

- Post the rotation schedule so students know when to move to the next center.

- The following suggestions will get you started. You will want to add any others for which you have special expertise.

Culminating Activities *(cont.)*

Debate and Discussion Centers

Several centers could be set up where students would formally present the debates they participated in during the project. They could also use their knowledge of debate to argue some of the great issues which faced the Founding Fathers, such as the conflict between large states and small states and the conflict between Northern and Southern states.

Speech Center

Students in this center could reprise the speeches they wrote or the famous speeches they delivered.

Philadelphia State House

Students can recreate the Philadelphia State House where the Constitutional Convention was held. You will need some pictures of the State House and supplies, including craft sticks for interior support, modeling clay, dirt, small pieces of fabric, felt, or construction paper.

Homes and Villages

Students can recreate colonial homes and villages using craft sticks, construction paper, glue, and other art materials.

Make a Franklin Kite

Use a center to create a simple kite using straws and tissue paper or other light materials. (Ben Franklin's contributions to science were almost as important as his other services to his country.)

Colonial Games

Games included foot races and variations of hide and seek. A sports center could feature relay races and one-on-one contests between students in the group.

Culminating Activities *(cont.)*

Map Making

A variety of maps could be created at this center. Use the map section of this book for examples and find others in atlases, encyclopedias, and the Internet. These maps would usually be done by small teams of two or three students. Maps of the 13 original states and maps of the expansion of the United States could be created. Maps could be drawn on tagboard, large construction paper, or built in three-dimensional form using clay or salt and flour.

Readers Theater

Students could create and produce their own Readers Theater presentations based on life in the new nation or events at the convention.

Literature Center

If your children read a literature selection together, you can set up a center to have them react to the selection. They could take the parts of various characters or simply choose to read a book about the same subject as a quiet break from the busy centers. Some possible selections are included in the Bibliography (page 61).

Other Centers

Other centers could include learning a square dance, weaving a simple pattern with yarn, knot tying, or a simple woodworking project.

Eat Hearty

If you have parent volunteers, plan a luncheon with an early American theme. Parents and students could do the decorations together. Most modern children are far more picky than their historical counterparts, but you might choose two or three dishes with an early American flavor.

Bibliography

Bjornlund, Lydia. *The U. S. Constitution: Blueprint for Democracy.* Lucent, 1999. (Written for able readers, this is a complete account of the Convention and the legacy of the Constitution.)

Collier, Christopher and James Lincoln. *Creating the Constitution, 1787.* Marshall Cavendish, 1999.

Catrow, David. *We the Kids: The Preamble to the Constitution of the United States.* Dial, 2002. (A nicely illustrated rendition of the preamble.)

Commanger, Henry Steele. *The Great Constitution: A Book for Young Americans.* Bobbs-Merrill, 1961. (A readable account told by one of the nation's leading historians.)

Faber, Doris and Harold. *We the People: The Story of the United States Constitution Since 1787.* Charles Scribner's Sons, 1987. (An excellent account of the changes in the Constitution over 200 years and the political and cultural causes.)

Johnson, Linda Carlson. *Our Constitution.* Millbrook Press, 1992.

Krull, Kathleen. *A Kid's Guide to America's Bill of Rights: Curfews, Censorship, and the 100-Pound Giant.* Avon, 1999. (Written for competent older students, this book details modern challenges to the first 10 amendments.)

Leebrick, Kristal. *The United States Constitution.* Capstone Press, 2002. (An easy introduction to the subject.)

Morris, Richard B. *The First Book of the Constitution.* Franklin Watts, 1958. (A simple but effective overview of the Constitution and the Convention by one of the nation's foremost historians.)

Patrick, John J. *The Young Oxford Companion to the Supreme Court of the United States.* Oxford University Press, 1994. (An excellent and complete volume on the Supreme Court for middle grade and high school students.)

Ritchie, Donald J. *The U. S. Constitution.* Chelsea House, 1989. (Good overall approach to the subject for middle grade readers.)

Sobel, Syl. *The U. S. Constitution and You.* Barron's, 2001.

Williams, Selma R. *Fifty-Five Fathers: The Story of the Constitutional Convention.* Dodd, Mead, 1970.

Glossary

affirmative—in a debate, the position which supports a resolution

amendment—a change to a legal document such as the Constitution

Articles of Confederation—the first leagle document which created a government of the United States before the Constitution came into existence

compromise—an agreement in which each side makes concessions

Constitution—the basic framework of laws in the United States

debate—a carefully prepared argument between individuals or teams

delegate—a person who represents others at a meeting

demigod—almost a god; a heroic figure

electoral college—the group of persons elected by the people to elect the President of the United States

executive—branch of government charged with enforcing laws

export—to ship out of a country

extemporaneous—public speaking without a written text

impeachment—the process of charging a government official with a crime; conviction brings the official's removal from office

implied powers—powers which are not actually written in the Constitution but which are implied within the document

import—to ship something into a country

insurrection—a rebellion, often with riots

judicial—the legal branch of government dealing with the courts

judicial review—the right of courts to review acts of a legislature or Congress to determine if they are in violation of the Constitution

legislative—the branch of government where the laws are written

negative—in a debate, the position which opposes the resolution

preamble—the introduction to a document such as the Constitution or the Declaration of Independence

ratification—the process of approving the Constitution or Constitutional amendments in each state

rebuttal—in a debate, a response to an opponent's statement

republic—as used by the delegates to the Constitutional Convention, a form of government in which the people exercise power rather than a king

segregation—to keep people separate from each other in schools, communities, and public facilities on the basis of race, color, nationality, or some other discriminating factor

senator—one of 100 members of the United States Senate

separation of powers—the division of government into three branches, legislative, executive and judicial, to prevent tyranny or misuse of power

sovereign—having the powers of a king

suffrage—the right to vote

tariff—a tax on exports or imports

taxes—money paid to support the functions of government

veto—a president's right to reject a law passed by Congress

Answer Key

Page 31

1. C	6. A
2. D	7. B
3. B	8. B
4. C	9. D
5. C	10. A

Page 32

1. B	6. D
2. A	7. D
3. D	8. A
4. B	9. D
5. B	10. B

Page 33

1. B	6. C
2. D	7. A
3. A	8. B
4. B	9. B
5. B	10. C

Page 34

1. D	6. A
2. A	7. B
3. B	8. B
4. D	9. A
5. A	10. B

Page 35

Supreme Court Decisions

D - F - A - C - B - E

Amendment Match

8 - 6 - 10 - 19 - 1 - 13 - 15–26 - 1 - 24 - 2 - 5 - 18 - 21–4 - 1 - 7 - 1 - 6 - 6 - 17 - 16–22 - 23

Page 37

State	Date Admitted Month/Year	Number of Representatives	Number of Senators
New Hampshire	June 1788	3	2
Massachusetts	February 1788	8	2
Rhode Island	May 1790	1	2
Connecticut	January 1788	5	2
New York	July 1788	6	2
New Jersey	December 1787	4	2
Pennsylvania	December 1787	8	2
Delaware	December 1787	1	2
Maryland	April 1788	6	2
Virginia	June 1788	10	2
North Carolina	November 1789	5	2
South Carolina	May 1788	5	2
Georgia	January 1788	3	2

2. Virginia
   Massachusetts
   Pennsylvania

3. Rhode Island
   Delaware

4. New York is located between the Northern and Southern states. It would have physically separated the nation.

Answer Key *(cont.)*

Page 38

1. California
2. Montana
   Wyoming
   Alaska
   North Dakota
   South Dakota
   Vermont
   Washington, D.C.
   Delaware
3. *11 states*

California	55
Texas	34
New York	31
Florida	27
Illinois	21
Pennsylvania	21
Ohio	20
Michigan	17
Georgia	15
North Carolina	15
New Jersey	15

   271 electoral votes
4. Idaho
   Maine
   New Hampshire
   Hawaii
   Rhode Island
5. Answers will vary.
6. Answers will vary.